PHILOSOPHICAL CRIMINOLOGY

NEW HORIZONS IN CRIMINOLOGY

PHILOSOPHICAL CRIMINOLOGY

Andrew Millie

First published in Great Britain in 2016 by

Policy Press
University of Bristol
1-9 Old Park Hill
Bristol
BS2 8BB
UK
t: +44 (0)117 954 5940
pp-info@bristol.ac.uk
www.policypress.co.uk

North America office:
Policy Press
c/o The University of Chicago Press
1427 East 60th Street
Chicago, IL 60637, USA
t: +1 773 702 7700
f: +1 773-702-9756
sales@press.uchicago.edu
www.press.uchicago.edu

British Library Cataloguing in Publication Data
A catalogue record for this book is available from the British Library

Library of Congress Cataloging-in-Publication Data
A catalog record for this book has been requested

ISBN 978-1-4473-2370-9 hardcover
ISBN 978-1-4473-2374-7 ePub
ISBN 978-1-4473-2375-4 Mobi

Cover design by Policy Press
Front cover image: istock
Printed and bound in Great Britain by CPI Group (UK) Ltd,
Croydon, CR0 4YY
Policy Press uses environmentally responsible print partners

For Lesley Millie

x

Contents

About the author

Andrew Millie is Professor of Criminology at Edge Hill University and Editor of Policy Press's *New Horizons in Criminology* book series. His current work explores the intersections between criminology and philosophy, human geography and theology. Andrew is also known for his work on policing and anti-social behaviour. His previous publications for Policy Press are *Securing Respect: Behavioural Expectations and Anti-Social Behaviour in the UK* (2009b), and the co-authored *Anti-Social Behaviour Strategies: Finding a Balance* (2005).

Acknowledgements

I am hugely thankful to my wife Lesley and children Ernest and Martha. I love you all to the moon and back. Maybe my next book will have more pictures (I know it's not a patch on *The Gruffalo*!) I also appreciate the support that I have from my mother, Joan Millie, as well as from various colleagues and friends. In particular, at Edge Hill University I want to thank Franco Rizzuto who has been happy for me to explore what is non-traditional territory for his department. It has been quite an adventure and at Edge Hill I am especially grateful for the encouragement of Janice Adams, Craig Collinson, Leon Culbertson and Chris Lawton. I also wish to thank Simon Mackenzie for our early discussions at the University of Glasgow on rules and criminology, and for helping to organise a joint panel with Richard Sparks at the 2009 British Society of Criminology Conference in Cardiff on 'Civility, criminology and philosophy'. Some of the ideas developed in this book had early outings in various articles and conference presentations. These are cited where appropriate. I am grateful for the support from Policy Press, especially from Alison Shaw, for encouraging me with my ideas for a 'New Horizons in Criminology' book series, and for the specific support and guidance from Rebecca Tomlinson and Victoria Pittman. Others who have helped me along the way include Jon Bannister, Karen Bullock, Rosie Erol, Victoria Herrington, Mike Hough and Karl Roberts. Many others deserve thanks and I apologise if I have missed anyone out. I wish to thank the anonymous reviewers who have helped to strengthen the manuscript and, finally, I wish to thank you for picking this book up. I hope you enjoy it!

Acknowledgements

NEW HORIZONS IN CRIMINOLOGY

Series editor: Professor Andrew Millie, Department of Law and Criminology, Edge Hill University, UK

Preface

Policy Press's New Horizons in Criminology book series provides concise authoritative texts that are international in scope and reflect cutting edge thought and theoretical developments. These short, accessible texts are written so that the nonspecialist academic, student or practitioner can understand them, by explaining principles and developments clearly before going deeper into the subject. Written by leading authors in their fields, the series will become essential reading for all academics and students (and practitioners) interested in where criminology is heading. The series was launched in 2016 with some great authors and important titles. The first books are: *Convict Criminology* by Rod Earle; *Indigenous Criminology* by Chris Cunneen and Juan Tauri; and *Sports Criminology* by Nic Groombridge. All three are highly recommended. Added to this is my own contribution on *Philosophical Criminology*. Other titles are in the pipeline.

The subject of criminology has always drawn on philosophical ideas, although this has often been on a pick-and-mix basis rather than a concerted engagement. As noted in this book's introduction, many criminologists would question the need for closer engagement with philosophy, and similarly not all philosophers will see the merit of engaging with criminology. Yet, the starting point for this book is that philosophers have for centuries been asking questions concerning how we get on with one another – and what happens when we do not – that have direct bearing on criminological concerns. Philosophers might also gain from greater exposure to the mess and dirt of the 'real world' as exposed by criminologists. Readers of this book will gain philosophical and theoretical insights into some big questions of direct relevance to criminology concerning values, morals, aesthetics, order/disorder, rules and respect. The book also highlights areas that are not often explored by criminologists, from landscape aesthetics through to theology. Examples are drawn from a variety of countries. My hope is that this book will become essential reading for those interested in questioning some of the underlying assumptions of the criminological enterprise.

ONE

A philosophical criminology

Introduction

This is a book about philosophy and criminology. There will be criminologists who question the need for closer engagement with philosophy and, likewise, philosophers who do not see a great deal of benefit from associating with criminology. My argument here is that philosophy is essential to criminology as philosophers have for centuries been asking questions concerning how we get on with one another – and what happens when we do not – that have direct bearing on criminological concerns. Philosophers might also gain from engagement with criminology and greater exposure to the messy and dirty 'real world'. For some the subject of criminology is simply a sociological or social policy interest. This book takes the view that criminology is much more than this, that there is also room for a philosophical criminology. I emphasise that this is 'a' philosophical criminology. Of course, there are many different philosophical standpoints as much as there are differing criminological perspectives, and it would be wrong to claim that this book presents the definitive philosophical criminology. Clearly I have my own views, values and preferred approaches which steer my writing. Thus, what this book contains is my take on a philosophical criminology. The reader is free to disagree. In fact, disagreement and debate are welcomed.

Some criminologists may consider the book a little esoteric for their particular view of the subject. Yet, take a look at most undergraduate criminology textbooks and there is a great deal of philosophy – although students may not always be aware of this. For instance, while it is often assumed that criminology originated in the 19th century with the dubious phrenology of Cesare Lombroso, textbook accounts also talk about an earlier 'classical criminology'. The enlightenment scholars cited – usually Jeremy Bentham and Cesare Beccaria, but also Thomas Hobbes, John Locke and Jean-Jacques Rousseau – were all philosophers rather than criminologists. Furthermore, more recent histories of criminology draw on an array of philosophical thought. For example, from the 19th century criminologists will be familiar with Émile Durkheim, Karl Marx and John Stuart Mill. From the 20th century there is criminological interest in the analytic philosophy tradition, such as the work of Richard Rorty (for example Wheeldon, 2015). There is also a lot of criminology that draws inspiration from various strands of continental thought, notably existentialism (for example Lippens and Crewe, 2011) and the works of Michel Foucault (especially *Discipline and Punish*, 1977). During the 1990s and beyond postmodern philosophy has had particular influence (for example Milovanovic, 1997); and in the 21st century critical criminologists may be influenced by Slavoj Žižek (for example 2008) and others. Over the past decade interest in a specifically philosophical criminology has grown, from Bruce Arrigo and Christopher Williams' (2006) excellent collection of essays on *Philosophy, Crime and Criminology*, through to Don Crewe and Ronnie Lippens' (2015) collection which drew on philosophy to ask *What is Criminology About?*. Most recently (2016) David Polizzi has taken a philosophical approach in considering phenomenology, social construction and social strain. From 2009 onwards David Polizzi has also been editor of the online *Journal of Theoretical and Philosophical Criminology*; and the journal *Criminal Law and Philosophy* (edited by Douglas Husak) also contains much criminological input. Rather than being an esoteric concern, it seems philosophical ideas permeate the criminological enterprise.

Philosophical criminology could be conceived as an applied philosophy, that it is the application of philosophy to a particular subject – 'crime'. However, there is a problem with such a conception. Philosophers tend to focus on certain aspects of the human condition such as logic, ethics, the mind, aesthetics or religion. It could be said that each of these is an applied philosophy – philosophical method and understanding applied to ethics, applied to aesthetics and so on. However, ethics is usually regarded as a philosophical concern and not an applied philosophical concern. There is no reason why this logic cannot be extended to other subjects of inquiry. Thus philosophy of history, philosophy of sport and political philosophy are all simply 'philosophy'. Similarly, philosophical criminology is simply philosophy as much as it is simply criminology.

This book aims to offer higher level content but written in an accessible style. The writings of some philosophers (and criminologists) can be impenetrable for the uninitiated. The hope with this book is to avoid this pitfall. The book develops a deepening understanding of such areas of philosophical enquiry that are relevant to the criminological context and reflects the international nature of the discipline. It builds on the author's own work in the UK and Canada on value judgements, aesthetics and respect (Millie, 2008; 2009a; 2011; 2016) as well as drawing from other nations and areas of philosophy.

In summary, readers will gain philosophical and theoretical insights into some big questions concerning how we get on with one another and what happens when we do not. Philosophy and criminology are both broad in terms of subjects studied and approaches taken. As such, the book is necessarily selective. It is structured around six areas of philosophical enquiry identified as important for criminological understanding, namely value judgements, morality, aesthetics, order/ disorder, rules and respect. Some other areas of philosophy relevant to criminology, such as the philosophy of punishment, are left as they are already amply covered elsewhere (for example Duff, 1986; Garland, 1990; Ellis, 2012). For this introductory chapter different strands of philosophical enquiry are considered and how they may relate to criminology. The chapter concludes by introducing the structure of the rest of the book. But first it is useful to consider what we mean by criminology and for this I use an analogy of a famous urinal that was submitted to an art exhibition in 1917.

Criminology, Marcel Duchamp and a urinal

In 1917 a submission entitled 'fountain' was entered into an exhibition of the Society of Independent Artists in New York. The 'fountain' in question was a porcelain urinal placed on its back and signed 'R. Mutt 1917'. It is usually attributed to Marcel Duchamp, although this authorship has been doubted by Julian Spalding and Glyn Thompson (The Jackdaw, 2015). In reply to Spalding and Thompson, and after assessing the evidence, the Director of the Tate Modern gallery in London, Nicholas Serota, stated that there is 'no reason to reattribute the work' (The Jackdaw, 2015). In the context of this book, whoever submitted the piece is less important than the fact that the urinal caused a scandal in the art world and became one of the biggest influences on 20th-century and contemporary art. According to Duchamp the urinal was a challenge to people's tastes and to the meaning of art: 'My fountain-urinal originated as an experiment in the matter of taste; I chose the object that was least likely to be liked. ... The danger is artistic pleasure. But you can still get people to swallow anything if you try, and that's what happened' (Duchamp, 1964, cited in Cabanne, 1997: 114).

Duchamp was part of the Dadaist movement, a group of avant-garde artists that questioned the meaning and substance of art. The urinal was what Duchamp called a 'readymade', with the art being in the choosing rather than in the craft of creating the piece. According to Pierre Cabanne (1997: 115) the urinal had demonstrated that 'anything could be "art", which meant, in its turn, that art could be any old thing'. Ever since, art for many people is whatever the artist calls art, or even whatever the viewer sees as art. There are also some who contend that something is art only if it is labelled as such by the institutions that comprise the artistic establishment. Why such cultural hierarchies should dictate tastes was explored by Pierre Bourdieu (1979/1984) and is considered further in Chapter Four on aesthetics. Whether defined by the artist, the viewer, or the institution, there is no objective 'thing' that makes something 'art'.

At first this may not appear too relevant to a discussion of criminology; however, my argument here is that contemporary criminology is similarly understood as so many different and diverse things that it too can be 'any old thing', and that anything could be criminological – although whether this is useful is another matter. Taken literally, 'criminology' is simply the study of crime. However, crime – and thus who is a criminal – is defined by law, a different subject area entirely. The relationship between criminology and law is an uneasy one; yet, according to Hans Boutellier (2000: 1), criminology is simply 'the social science that addresses conduct relevant to criminal law'. Similarly, for American criminologists Edwin Sutherland and Donald Cressey (1955: 3) criminology is concerned with 'the processes of making laws, of breaking laws, and of reacting towards the breaking of laws'. Stanley Cohen (1988: 9) rephrased this as: 'Why are laws made? Why are they broken? What do we do or what should we do about this?' (see also Young, 1981). There is a clear logical relationship between criminology and criminal law. That said, according to Ian Loader and Richard Sparks (2011: 26) there are difficulties in answering questions 'concerning the work criminologists can and should do, the problems that are selected for attention, the methods deployed to solve them, and the audiences towards which such activity is addressed'. In short, contemporary criminology is interested in much more than criminal law and perhaps has more in common with modern and contemporary art in covering 'any old thing'.

British criminologist David Downes famously claimed that criminology is a rendezvous subject (Garland and Sparks, 2000), that it is a meeting place for ideas from a range of disciplines as applied to the problem of crime. What constitutes a crime is generally recognised as being socially constructed (through law) and it changes depending on time, place and culture. Defining actions or omissions as 'crimes' is done by those with power, leaving the powerless to discover aspects of their existence criminalised. For critical criminologists the primary definer is the state. Due to the relationship between criminalisation and power – whether from the state, corporations or others with power – some criminologists prefer to jettison criminology's reliance on crime and criminals altogether, instead focusing on deviancy or harm, although these subjects themselves draw from other disciplines – notably politics and sociology, as well as law. In recent years the study of deviancy has in part evolved into a cultural criminology emphasising resistance, risk taking and play (Ferrell and Sanders, 1995). The study of harm or zemiology (Hillyard et al, 2004) draws specific inspiration from John Stuart Mill's 'harm principle'; as stated in *On Liberty*: 'The only purpose for which power can be rightfully exercised over any member of a civilized community, against his will, is to prevent harm to others. His own good, either physical or moral, is not a sufficient warrant' (Mill, 1859/2002: 8).

The legal philosopher Joel Feinberg has extended this by examining how the law is used to prevent harm to others (1984) and harm to self (1986). In considering the possibility of harmless wrongdoing (1990: xxvii), Feinberg observed that harm is 'a treacherous word'; it is 'both vague and ambiguous, and entangled with other concepts, like "wrong", in ordinary usage'. What is considered 'wrong' or 'right' is a moral concern and is considered more fully in the chapters that follow. But sticking with 'harm' for now, what I consider harmful behaviour may be quite different to what you call harmful, and it may change depending on context. Furthermore, drawing on Feinberg, there may be differences in what we perceive as harmless wrongdoing as well as wrong-less harm. Like crime, harm is clearly a social construction. By shifting criminology's attention to harm – or similarly to deviancy – it is possible that one contested concept (crime) is simply replaced by another. The focus of criminology becomes an ever more slippery fish. It is little surprise that in an undergraduate piece of work that I once marked the view was expressed that 'criminology aims to understand and explain why people do certain things and behave in a certain way'. This was so vague that it was meaningless; but was the student necessarily wrong? My feedback to the student was that their statement was also true of a number of other disciplines and subject areas. Is criminology so vague that it is concerned with crime, deviance or harm, or perhaps non-normative behaviour, incivility, morally repugnant or offensive behaviour, or whatever we find objectionable or wrong, or simply bad? Following Duchamp the focus of criminology becomes whatever we want it to be (or whatever others expect criminologists to be studying). In effect, criminology becomes the study of the 'bad stuff' that happens – a sort of bad-ology that recognises that one person's 'bad stuff' will be tolerated or even celebrated elsewhere.

While some criminologists do not like to talk about crime, others publishing in criminology journals would rather be known by other academic labels, be they socio-legal scholars, sociologists, economists, geographers, psychologists or zemiologists. Furthermore, while some focus on harms through zemiology – or what Clifford Shearing (2015) has labelled harm-ology – other criminologists turn their attention to risk or security (for example Valverde, 2014) in what could be seen as risk-ology or security-ology (see Shearing, 2015). Mariana Valverde (2013) has wondered how far criminological research can drift 'from the central notion of crime ... before leaving criminology altogether' (cited in Shearing, 2015: 264). The budding criminologist is left wondering, what's left, and does criminology have an identity crisis?

A state of crisis in criminology is nothing new. Much of the 1960s' and '70s' sociology of deviance or 'anti-criminology' (see Cohen, 1988) was in direct opposition to the perceived dominance of positivism and, in Britain in particular, criminology's relationship with the state; but, as Stanley Cohen famously put it: 'Every attempt I have ever made to distance myself from the subject, to criticize it, even to question its very right to exist, has only got me more involved in its inner life. ... To be against criminology, it seems, one has to be part of it' (Cohen, 1988: 8).

Returning to Duchamp, perhaps criminology has evolved to a position where an academic 'does' criminology if that is how they label their work, irrespective of content – in effect, I call myself a criminologist, therefore what I do is criminology. My own view is that, while the study of 'crime' and 'criminals' may be imperfect, it does at least give the subject a core focus. Criminologists can then move away from this core to investigate harms (Hillyard et al., 2004), deviancy (Atkinson, 2014) or broader 'problem behaviours' (Gottfredson, 2011). Other will no doubt disagree.

Whatever criminology is, it is a huge and popular subject. Over the past half century growth has been so extensive that there are very few universities in the English-speaking world that do not offer study in criminology at postgraduate and/or undergraduate levels. Growth has also occurred elsewhere, notably with European and Asian criminologies. African and South American criminologies are also developing (Bosworth and Hoyle, 2011). According to Jock Young (2003: 97) 'it is a subject where other disciplines meet and its very liveliness and, at its best, intellectual interest is because of its position on the busy crossroads of sociology, psychology, law and philosophy'. Being at such a crossroads it is understandable that there are differences of opinion regarding the focus of the subject. Other disciplinary influences can be added to Young's list, including: politics (Amatrudo, 2009); economics (Albertson and Fox, 2012); geography (Weisburd et al, 2012); history (Godfrey et al, 2008); cultural studies and literature (O'Neill and Seal, 2012); theology (Bottoms and Preston, 1980); biology (Walsh, 2009); social policy (Knepper, 2007); architecture (Simon et al, 2013); and urban design (Newman, 1972). You may think of others to add to this list.

In short, criminology is the application of other disciplines to the study of crime and criminals (and also deviance, harm, incivility, offence and so on, depending on your take on the subject). According to David Garland (2011) criminology lacks a unifying epistemology and is not in itself a discipline at all. It is a subject area that is often housed within a range of other academic departments, including sociology, law, criminal justice and social policy. This is not necessarily a problem. Other subjects are taught at university which are based on the topic under consideration rather than a particular disciplinary approach. And there is a lot to be said for approaching a topic from a range of angles; as Young asserts, this variety adds to a subject's 'very liveliness' (2003: 97). It also leaves open the possibility of inter- and trans-disciplinary learning. Of course, there are some criminologists who reside in epistemological, ontological and disciplinary bunkers, a problem not unique to criminology. There is a Balkanisation within criminology with some criminologists being intolerant of other positions. Some may be so sold on their particular vision of criminology that they see their brand as the *only* way forward. For instance, according to Pat Carlen (2011: 95–96), '... it is unfortunate that three of the most exciting perspectives in criminology today – those academy-based criminologies which have variously self-branded as "critical", "cultural" or "public" – at times reveal evangelistic tendencies that pose a threat to their capacity for the open debate that each of them espouses'.

A consideration for this book is what can be learned through such open debate by looking outside the bunker, in particular towards philosophy. The discipline of philosophy has similarly suffered divides and schisms and criminology can learn from the experience of philosophy in this regard. But more generally, criminologists can learn a great deal from philosophy, which has for centuries been asking similar questions concerning how we get on with one another.

I take as a starting point a divide in philosophy that occurred from Immanuel Kant onwards, often characterised as a split between analytic and continental philosophy. Like Simon Critchley (2001) I take a view that, at their extremes, analytic philosophy has the risk of scientism, regarding scientific method as applicable to all problems. Conversely, continental philosophy risks becoming unintelligible obscurantism. For example, a letter was famously published in *The Times* in 1992 signed by a number of philosophers criticising an honorary degree being given to Jacques Derrida by the University of Cambridge:

> M. Derrida's voluminous writings in our view stretch the normal forms of academic scholarship beyond recognition. Above all – as every reader can very easily establish for himself (and for this purpose any page will do) – his works employ a written style that defies comprehension. Many have been willing to give M. Derrida the benefit of the doubt, insisting that language of such depth and difficulty of interpretation must hide deep and subtle thoughts indeed. When the effort is made to penetrate it, however, it becomes clear, to us at least, that, where coherent assertions are being made at all, these are either false or trivial. (Smith et al, 1992)

Both scientism and obscurantism diminish the influence and importance of a subject. As John Stuart Mill is cited as saying, 'the one doctrine is accused of making men beasts, the other lunatics' (cited in Critchley, 2001: 7). Similarly for criminology, there is a risk of seeing crime and its control as a science but also of creating a discipline that is so impenetrable and obscure that it has little or no relevance nor usefulness for people's everyday experiences. But before going further it is worthwhile to consider the analytic and continental traditions in philosophy.

Criminology and analytic and continental philosophy

When giving feedback on student work a common comment is that an essay gives a good description of the problem, but lacks critique, or that the student shows some knowledge of the subject but not critical understanding. There is a divide between knowing and understanding and in philosophy this is reflected in a divide between knowledge and wisdom. Ancient philosophy clearly emphasised a search for wisdom. For instance, for Socrates wisdom concerned what it might mean to lead a good human life. For Aristotle the emphasis was on the meaning of happiness. Yet in late modern society – and especially in academia

– knowledge is often regarded as more important than wisdom with individual and societal progress measured by how much we know; as Francis Bacon is alleged to have said, 'knowledge is power'. The Latin for knowledge is *scientia* and the search for knowledge is a scientific one. It is the job of the natural sciences to offer empirical and testable proof. For some criminologists this is also the job of criminology. In fact from 2001 onwards some criminologists in Britain have preferred to be known as crime scientists.[1] According to one of its founders, Gloria Laycock (2005: 4), crime science is 'the application of the methods of science to crime and disorder'. Laycock went further:

> ... rather like medical science, it is seen as outcome-focused. It is about reducing crime, as medical science is about reducing ill health. ... Crime science is also multi-disciplinary in that the physical, social, biological and computer sciences are all seen as relevant to crime control, and therefore to crime science. (Laycock, 2005: 6)

Medicalised models of research are often given greatest weight with random-controlled trials regarded as the gold standard for research in what has been seen as an experimental turn in criminology (see Hough, 2010; Sampson, 2010). Scientific enquiry has been central to criminology from the 19th century onwards. For instance, undergraduate criminologists are often taught that early examples of positivist criminology include the scientific use of crime statistics by Adolphe Quetelet (see for example Beirne, 1987) and the phrenology of Cesare Lombroso – who Paul Knepper and Per Jørgen Ystehede describe as 'the single most important figure in the founding of criminology' (2013: i). Yet for others criminology is not a science and a definitive cause of crime cannot be found, even if a definitive definition of crime were possible in the first place. The social world is not a Petri dish where crimes and criminals (and potential crimes and criminals) can be scientifically analysed. My own view on criminology is that there is room for scientific method but not at the expense of other forms of enquiry. Furthermore, the subjectivity and social construction of crime, deviance and harm have to be acknowledged.

But if knowledge is king then other disciplines and subject areas – including criminology and philosophy – are in service to the scientific project. According to John Locke (1689/1995) in his *An Essay Concerning Human Understanding*, philosophy is such an under-labourer or handmaiden to science. Philosophy is in effect relegated to epistemology, a theory of knowledge. In this guise knowledge is gained through exact and impersonal scientific study of logic and language. For fear of simplification this is broadly the view of the Anglo-American analytic tradition which, drawing on mathematics, emerged at the start of the 20th century with Bertrand Russell, Ludwig Wittgenstein, Gottlob Frege and others. Yet some philosophers would take offence, arguing that human experience is far from exact. According to Critchley (2001: 3):

> In my view, the problem here is not so much with people outside philosophy as with people inside philosophy, our professional [analytic] philosophers. For most of us, the very idea that philosophy might be concerned with the question of the meaning of life or the attainment of a good and happy human life is something of a joke, and furthermore a joke in rather poor taste.

For Critchley, analytic philosophy's emphasis on science and knowledge means the search for wisdom becomes relegated to 'folk psychology'. Since its inception analytic philosophy has picked up various influences along the way, including the logical positivism of Rudolf Carnap and others emphasising a need for logical or empirical verification. Today, not only is analytic philosophy the dominant form of Anglo-American philosophical enquiry, it is also the dominant influence on Anglo-American positivist criminology and crime science.

Yet, as noted, many criminologists see criminology as something other than a scientific enquiry and consider experiences of crime, harm and deviance to be subjective. The main influence for such non-positivistic criminology is the continental school of philosophy, which has attempted to bridge the divide between knowledge and wisdom. This was done by focusing on what Arthur Schopenhauer saw as the problem of existence – that we as humans all die, and we are aware of this. This is the grounding for existentialism and suitable subjects for philosophical enquiry become the meaning of life, issues of personal character, the meaning of suffering and the importance of beauty. Continental philosophy covers a broad range of philosophical enquiry but principally centres on existentialism and phenomenology – the study of subjective experience. Most continental philosophers would not argue that science is wrong, but that science might not be best equipped to answer existential questions.

Continental philosophy is broadly hermeneutic in approach in that it is interested in written, verbal and non-verbal communication. It is interested in social critique and is contextualist in emphasising context in order to understand a problem. This context might be historical, structural, cultural, spatial, temporal or have any number of other influencing factors. The label 'continental philosophy' did not come to prominence until the mid-20th century and so many philosophers who fit under the label – such as Friedrich Nietzsche, Martin Heidegger, Jean-Paul Sartre, Jacques Derrida, Michel Foucault, and so on – would not necessarily have seen themselves this way. That said, the label was used in the 1840s by John Stuart Mill in two essays comparing the romanticism of Samuel Taylor Coleridge with the utilitarianism of Jeremy Bentham, what he described as Kantian-influenced continental philosophers compared to the English empiricism of Bentham and others (see Critchley, 2001). To simplify Mill's position, Bentham asked 'is it true?' whereas Coleridge wanted to know, 'what is the meaning of it?' (Critchley, 2001: 42). For instance, a scientific/analytic approach to violence might be to study the brain in search of serotonin imbalances. An alternative (continental) search for meaning might consider what it feels like to be violent or to be violently victimised, or perhaps what it means to be labelled as violent.

The simplistic division between analytic and continental philosophy is between philosophy as science or as art. But according to Hugh McDonald (2004: xii) philosophy is neither:

> The [analytic] handmaiden role, the envy of physics, and the Continental attempt to reduce philosophy to fable are indeed the prelude to the death of such philosophy ... The idea never seems to have occurred to these philosophers that maybe philosophy is neither a science nor an art. That perhaps philosophy is a field without a rival, *sui generis*.

Of course it is easy to paint a picture of divides whereas the reality is that some analytic philosophers have more in common with the continental tradition and vice versa. For instance, Ludwig Wittgenstein, who is usually seen as an analytic philosopher, was unsympathetic to the notion that philosophical problems could be solved by the natural sciences. Similarly, within criminology there are some that are labelled as crime scientists or 'administrative criminologists' who recognise the subjectivity of crime and that science has its limitations. There are also critical criminologists who are more than happy to adopt scientific/ quantitative method. Like philosophy, criminology and criminologists are not easy to categorise (but neither should they be).

The structure of this book

The rest of this book considers six aspects of philosophical enquiry that are directly relevant to criminological concerns. These are value judgements, morality, aesthetics, order/disorder, rules and respect. Given the breadth of philosophy I have had to be selective. There are, of course, many other areas of philosophy of relevance to criminology. For instance, I have not considered the philosophy of sentencing, punishment or justice. While exceptionally important, these are covered at length elsewhere. Instead, I wanted to focus on other equally important areas of philosophy that have a direct bearing on debates within criminology.

In this introduction the distinction between continental and analytic philosophy has been outlined. While differences exist, especially at their extremes, there is some crossover between the two traditions with philosophers drawing ideas from both. Similarly, criminology is perhaps at its best when it is open to ideas, rather than painted into a corner. Thus, this book draws from both continental and analytic traditions. However, there is particular emphasis on Kantian ideas concerning human dignity. Relatedly the book also draws on ideas concerning the Golden Rule and Paul Ricoeur's (1990) work on Christian theology and an 'economy of gift' (see, for instance, Chapter Three).

Chapter Two focuses on the value judgements that are made, both by criminologists and by the rest of society, in determining which actions or omissions are celebrated, tolerated or censured as unacceptable. It is contended that the same behaviours can be celebrated in one context, but censured elsewhere. Different moral, aesthetic, prudential and economic value judgements are considered. Moral philosophy is looked at in more depth in Chapter Three. In line with the British criminologist Anthony Bottoms (2002: 24), it is contended that 'all criminologists have to be interested in morality'. The chapter considers different philosophical traditions focusing on virtues, consequences and deontological notions of duty and rules. Criminology's historic association with utilitarian thinking is highlighted; but then the chapter concludes by considering in more detail the Golden Rule and Immanuel Kant's categorical imperative.

Chapter Four focuses on aesthetics. For some the link between aesthetics and criminology might not be immediately apparent. However, what this chapter demonstrates is that people's aesthetic expectations can determine what is regarded as acceptable behaviour, or whose presence is tolerated in public spaces. Aesthetics can also, for example, have a bearing on which graffiti writers become celebrities and which end up in prison. Furthermore, ideas of landscape beauty can lead to the criminalisation of people or things that do not fit in. In this regard, aesthetics could be very important for criminology.

The focus for Chapter Five is order and disorder. The importance of social order – and how it can be maintained – is considered along with how we can live together at a time when late-modern individualism dictates that we should put ourselves first. Most criminologists will be familiar with work on anomie, especially by Émile Durkheim and Robert Merton. And some will also draw on postmodern perspectives on chaos. Both anomie and chaos theory are examined. Building on Chapter Four the notion of an aesthetic order is also considered.

Chapter Six focuses on normative and legal rules that are put in place to make an ordered society more of a possibility. Politicians are keen to highlight their support for people who 'play by the rules'. The extent to which people actually play by the rules is questioned, and the degree to which rules are bent or exceptions to rules are found is highlighted. Social contract theory is explored as well as the possibility that the morally right thing to do might sometimes be to break the law.

Chapter Seven considers the topic of respect and draws on Kant's notion of dignity and of treating humans as ends and not means to an end. Such egalitarianism where respect is due to all persons is contrasted with the alternative view that respect has to be earned. The final conclusions chapter brings the findings of the book together and contemplates the possibility of an empathetic criminology. The chapter finishes with a reflection on the exercise of putting 'a' philosophical criminology together.

Note

[1]   In 2001 the Jill Dando Institute of Crime Science (since rebranded as the Jill Dando Institute of Security and Crime Science) was established at University College London led by Gloria Laycock, the former Head of the Policing and Reducing Crime Unit at the UK Home Office.

TWO

Value judgements

Introduction

The sociologist Howard Becker once claimed that value-neutral sociology is not possible, that a person's research cannot be divorced from their personal beliefs and values. The same is true for philosophy, criminology and, arguably, all other academic disciplines – despite some academics' claims that their research is value free. According to Becker:

> ... one would have to assume, as some apparently do, that it is indeed possible to do research that is uncontaminated by personal and political sympathies. I propose to argue that it is not possible and, therefore, that the question is not whether we should take sides, since we inevitably will, but rather whose side we are on (Becker, 1967: 239).

Becker was asking for a value judgement to be made regarding an appropriate moral position for academic research. The answer for many sociologists has been that they are on the side of the oppressed, the downtrodden, the 'other'. Much of criminology – especially that which calls itself critical – has claimed a similar allegiance; as the critical criminologist Phil Scraton (2005: 23) has put it: 'It is about bearing witness, gathering testimonies, sharing experiences, garnering the view from below and exposing the politics and discourses of authoritarianism.' Scraton's assessment is a clear value judgement of the purpose of critical scholarship. It is about social justice, it is anti-authoritarian and it is political. Of course, deciding which particular voices are 'from below' is itself a value judgement. At the other end of the spectrum much of Anglo-American criminology is positivist, seeing criminology as a science where the criminologist's job is to be as impartial as possible (see for example Tonry, 2014; Gelsthorpe, 2015). Yet impartiality is an impossibility; criminologists of all persuasions make value judgements concerning what they consider important to study as well as the theories and methods they choose to adopt.

Similarly, value judgements are central to what societies, governments and individuals regard as acceptable or unacceptable behaviour, what

– or who – ought to be criminalised, what is regarded as serious or non-serious criminality, how to police, whether or not (or how) to punish and what might constitute a solution to 'the crime problem'. The fact that our values differ will mean that ideas of criminality and criminological solutions may also vary substantially, as highlighted by the Chicago School sociologist Louis Wirth (1931: 484–5):

> Whatever may be the physical, the psychological and the temperamental differences between various races and societies, one thing is certain, namely that their cultures are different. Their traditions, their modes of living and making a living, the values that they place upon various types of conduct are often so strikingly different that what is punished as a crime in one group is celebrated as heroic conduct in another.

Put simply, what I consider to be unacceptable or criminal behaviour may be tolerated or even celebrated elsewhere (Millie, 2011). It is my contention that value judgements are thus critical to criminological concerns. A more specific example is given by the philosopher Carl Wellman (1975: 80) when talking about marijuana use:

> To argue that marijuana is good because it gives pleasure or is a means to knowledge, for example, presupposes that pleasure and knowledge are good. On the other hand, to argue that marijuana is bad because it causes automobile accidents or crime tacitly assumes that accidents and crime are bad. The soundness of each argument, then, depends in part upon the correctness of the value judgment or judgments it takes for granted.

Value judgements influence debates on both the legalisation and criminalisation of drugs. These debates centre on individual and societal liberty and issues concerning harm to self and harm to others (Feinberg, 1984; 1986). There are, of course, arguments concerning the extent to which the state ought to adopt paternal interest in individuals' lives. There is also a view that drug use is simply immoral as it impedes rationality and autonomy. According to Paul Smith (2008) this is a Kantian take on drug use, although such a judgement would apply to legal as well as illegal drugs. Smith concedes that Kant thought that moderate alcohol use and medical opium were 'permissible'. Furthermore, according to Smith (2008: 9) 'one can, without self-contradiction, rationally and autonomously choose to do something that reduces or even ends one's rationality and autonomy'. This may be debated. There are additional arguments concerning the offensiveness of drug consumption, the law's role in promoting virtue and prohibiting vice, and the preservation of a traditional way of life reflecting majoritarian judgement. There is no simple explanation for why something – in this case drug use – is deemed to be wrong; yet such assessments are clearly influenced by our values.

This chapter explores such value judgements by drawing on the philosophy of values or axiology (which is sometimes referred to as value theory). Returning to Howard Becker (1963: 129–30), he once noted that: 'Specific rules find their beginnings in those vague and generalized statements of preference social scientists often call values. Scholars have proposed many varying definitions of value, but we need not enter that controversy here.'

This chapter sees values as fundamental to criminology and that it is essential to 'enter that controversy'. Axiology is most often associated with *evaluative* moral judgements of what is good and bad. Drawing on deontological ethics (see Zimmerman, 2015) there are also *deontic* moral judgements of rightness, wrongness, obligation, requirement, reason for doing and what ought to be. There are additionally aesthetic value judgements regarding what is considered beautiful, ugly or perhaps just aesthetically inappropriate. Both moral and aesthetic value judgements are considered in this chapter but are also looked at in more detail in the chapters that follow. Alongside moral and aesthetic judgements, this chapter argues that prudential and economic value judgements are also important for processes of criminalisation (Millie, 2011).

Axiology

The analytic philosopher GE Moore once intuitively claimed that 'Good is good, and that is the end of the matter' (1903/2005: 7). Moore's understanding of conceptual analysis was that complex concepts are divided into simpler parts and analysed. For Moore, 'goodness' is viewed as a simple concept that cannot be divided and is therefore unanalysable, 'that is the end of the matter'. Moore's position is neatly summarised by Judith Jarvis Thomson (1997: 273): 'Moore's story begins with the good. Some things are good, Moore said, and some things are not good; so there is such a property as goodness – all good things have it and all things that are not good lack it.' Writing in 1903 Moore took the view that 'goodness' is the only unanalysable ethical concept: 'That which is meant by "good" is in fact, except its converse "bad", the *only* simple object of thought which is peculiar to Ethics' (1903/2005: 57, emphasis in original). However by 1912 he concluded that some deontic concepts were also unanalysable, such as rightness, duty and obligation (see Olson, 2015: 47).

For WD Ross (1930/2002) Moore's use of the word 'good' is *predictive* – that, for example, by saying that pleasure is good we are claiming that pleasure is good absolutely, rather than relative to something else. Alternatively, by saying that someone is a good dancer or a good painter we are making claims to goodness relative to something else (dancing and painting); and for Ross this is an *attributive* use of the word 'good'. Axiology is concerned with both predictive and attributive uses of 'good' (for example Lemos, 1995; Griffin, 1996; Rønnow-Rasmussen and Zimmerman, 2005; Rønnow-Rasmussen, 2015; Zimmerman, 2015). It is also concerned with other uses of 'good', such as the difference between describing a view as good and describing someone's behaviour as good. There are aesthetic consequences of the former and moral consequences of the latter. With the example of a good view, if something or someone is deemed to impede this view then they may be forcibly removed, be they residents of an illegal traveller camp removed from a rural parkland or homeless people from an urban retail district. There can therefore be also moral (and maybe criminal) consequences of aesthetic value judgements.

In philosophical writings on value there is often also a distinction made between something having intrinsic value (it is good in itself) or extrinsic value (good in relation to other things of value). There are some who question an intrinsic–extrinsic distinction (for example Geach, 1956; Thomson, 1997; Kraut, 2011; see also Olson, 2015). According to Peter Geach (1956), for example, good can only be described relative to something else (extrinsically). However, a popular argument for intrinsic goodness centres on the creation story in Genesis (Butchvarov, 1989; Kraut, 2011). According to Richard Kraut, for example:

> Recall the familiar words of the book of Genesis: On the first day of creation, 'God said "let there be light": And there was light. And God saw the light, that it was good' (1:31). Several lines later, after God has created the dry lands and the seas, he again contemplates his creation, and sees that it was good. ... Genesis does not say that God saw his work was good *for* someone. There was no one, just yet, for whom the light and the division of land and sea was good. The Bible depicts the newly created world as

something that is, quite simply, good. ... God is supremely and absolutely good – not good in relation to something else, but just plain good. Little wonder, then, that what he makes will also be good (period). (2011: 12–13, emphasis in original)

For Kraut the concept of intrinsic goodness has coherence, although there may be limitations when applying it to our everyday lived experiences. However, the use of the word 'good' in the story may also mean that creation was good for whom it was intended, namely us; as Jonas Olson (2015: 53) has similarly noted: 'God saw ... that what he had created was good to look at, or perhaps more plausibly, that it was good for the alleged crown of his creation, namely human beings'. Thus even in this case the word 'good' may be being used extrinsically rather than intrinsically. Perhaps a clearer example of absolute/intrinsic goodness is provided in the gospel of Mark (10:17–18),[1] according to which: 'As Jesus started on his way, a man ran up to him and fell on his knees before him. "Good teacher," he asked, "what must I do to inherit eternal life?" "Why do you call me good?" Jesus answered. "No one is good – except God alone."'[2]

Jesus challenges the questioner to think through the implications of calling him 'good teacher'. The view here is that *only* God is 'good' – and if Jesus is good then he must also be God. The context of the passage is that the questioner is trying his best to be as good as he can, but falls short. The challenge for him is to follow Jesus, the only true example of goodness. In living our everyday lives we exhibit goodness – extrinsic goodness and maybe a degree of intrinsic goodness as reflective of God; but we also exhibit a fair amount of badness. Of course there are many who do not believe in a deity and for whom this example will make less sense. The important point is that while there is such a thing as extrinsic goodness, intrinsic or absolute goodness may be harder to come by.

Axiology and everyday life

According to Judith Jarvis Thomson (1997: 276) 'all goodness is goodness in a way'. Examples given included: being good with children, good to look at, good in Hamlet, or something being good for people. Most significantly, she thought there was no such thing as 'plain, pure good' (Thomson, 2001: 19; see also Olson, 2015). Similarly, JL Mackie (1977: 15) proposed a moral scepticism, stating that 'There are no objective values'. He went further, claiming that all evaluative and deontic judgements of moral value as well as aesthetic judgements are subjective:

> The claim that values are not objective, are not part of the fabric of the world, is meant to include not only moral goodness, which might be most naturally equated with moral value, but also other things that could be more loosely called moral values or disvalues – rightness and wrongness, duty, obligation, an action's being rotten and contemptible, and so on. It also includes non-moral values, notably aesthetic ones, beauty and various kinds of artistic merit (1977: 15).

The position taken in this book is less sceptical with the view that objective 'plain, pure good' and intrinsic value are possibilities – especially if there is a God; however, what Thomson and Mackie have rightly highlighted is the subjectivity of much that we value and call 'good' in our everyday lives. For instance, using Thomson's examples, whether something or someone is good to look at is entirely personal; similarly, determining who is good at Hamlet, or what is good for someone can be similarly subjective. Thus, rather than focus on intrinsic and extrinsic value it might be more useful for everyday life to consider how we perceive, evaluate and value goodness (as well as deontic moral concepts such as rightness, obligation, requirement and ought).

It is possible that each of us values certain 'goods' *as though* they are intrinsically good, irrespective of whether they are good absolutely. There may be such a thing as absolute goodness, but if we treat something as though it is intrinsically good, at that moment, to all intents and purposes, it becomes absolutely good for us. Similarly, there may be actions or omissions that are treated as though absolutely bad – such as rape or slavery – that are morally wrong at any time and in any circumstances. Yet, if those with power treat them otherwise then even rape and slavery become negotiable for them (Millie, 2011).

At this point some scholars would propose a version of 'relative truth' or metaethical relativism, which, according to Carson and Moser (2001: 2), simply states that 'what is true for one person (or society) might not be true for another person (or society)'. This view builds on Friedrich Nietzsche's contention that 'There are no moral phenomena at all, only a moral interpretation of phenomena' (1886/2003: 96). An example is provided by criminologists Erich Goode and Nachman Ben-Yehuda (2009: 111) with adulterers being stoned in Iran, but within Sikhism being 'tolerated, often encouraged and even, upon occasion, rewarded'. Thus what is morally true for Iranian nationals is not morally true for religious Sikhs. This relativism would become muddied for a Sikh who happened to be living in Iran. Such relativism can be either individual or cultural. In philosophy there is also a distinction made between agent relativism (the relativism of an agent performing an action) and appraiser relativism (the relativism of someone forming a moral judgement about somebody's action) (see Lyons, 1976; Sturgeon, 1994). A critical realist perspective (for example Bhaskar, 1975; Archer et al, 1998) is that relativism denies the possibility of an objective or universal reality. Furthermore, if everything is relative then one cannot be proved wrong. According to Harry Gensler and Earl Tokmenko (2004) cultural relativism divides people between different cultures and therefore limits cross-cultural learning. Furthermore:

> [Cultural relativism] says that whatever is socially approved must thereby be good. So if it's socially good to value money above all else, then this must be good. And if it's socially approved to put Jews in concentration camps, then this too must be good. To live as a cultural relativist is to live as an uncritical conformist. But cultural relativism is an error: 'good' doesn't mean 'socially approved'. What is socially approved may sometimes be very bad. (Gensler and Tokmenko, 2004: 56)

An alternative to relativism is universalism, which, according to Julia Driver (2007: 17), is the idea that 'at least some basic moral norms and values are universal' (2007: 17). In comparing universalism to relativism Driver considers the morality of female circumcision:

> This is the practice, in some cultures, of excising a portion of the female genitalia. It is usually practiced on young girls. It is quite painful and can lead to numerous health problems for the girls, but is practiced for cultural reasons and, some argue, as a way of depriving females of sexual enjoyment. Of course, in Western cultures such a practice is considered quite immoral, so here we have a case of cultural moral disagreement. Moral relativism would hold that in Western cultures 'Female circumcision is wrong' is true, whereas in cultures where people don't happen to hold similar beliefs that claim would be false, and it may well be true instead that 'Female circumcision is right', (2007: 18)

Put another way, a relativist view would hold that what is constructed as true for me may not be true for you. However, in the case of female circumcision – or perhaps torture, slavery, racism, paedophilia, genocide, and so on – a universalist argument would be that they are always wrong. According to Driver (2007) cultural differences do not disprove the possibility of universal truth. Claims for moral universalism are normative or prescriptive claims that 'people ought to abide by these norms', rather than descriptive claims 'that they do in fact abide by these norms' (2007: 19). Even if they were descriptive claims, it could be circumstances or non-moral beliefs, rather than values that differ. Karl Popper's (1945: 53) critique of relativism centred on what he saw as a misunderstanding of the statement that 'norms are man-made[3] (in the sense that the responsibility for them is entirely ours)'. According to Popper:

> Nearly all misunderstandings can be traced back to one fundamental misapprehension, namely, to the belief that 'convention' implies 'arbitrariness'; that if we are free to choose any system of norms we like, then one system is just as good as any other. ... But artificiality by no means implies full arbitrariness. Mathematical calculi, for instance, or symphonies, or plays, are highly artificial, yet it does not follow that one calculus or symphony or play is just as good as any other. Man has created new worlds of music, of poetry, of science, and the most important of these is the world of the moral demands for equality, for freedom, and for helping the weak. (1945: 53–4)

In comparing morals to music or poetry, Popper noted that, while art is a matter of taste, moral decisions are much more important: 'Many moral decisions involve the life and death of other men. Decisions in the field of art are much less urgent and important' (1945: 54). Here I take a contextually constructivist position (Millie, 2011) where both context and power are important determinants for what is generally regarded or constructed as valuable or valueless, as good or bad. It is a normative ethical position that recognises the universalism that some things are – or perhaps should be – always good (and some are always bad); but it is the construction of goodness and badness that has a more immediate impact on our everyday lives. For criminological understanding this is a particularly useful way of thinking. If something such as pleasure is generally perceived, constructed and valued as intrinsically good then something else – such as pain – can generally be viewed as intrinsically bad. In simple terms, actions or omissions that bring about pain might qualify for censure and criminalisation. For example, various forms of crime are constructed as extrinsically bad as they lead to pain and are therefore censurable. Returning to the earlier example of a 'good' view, the travellers or homeless people who obstruct this view are perceived as extrinsically valueless and are removed and criminalised as they hinder something else that is regarded of value. Yet there may be things more important to value than a good view, including the liberty of those removed.

Across liberal democracies there are frequent calls to adhere to 'the values of the majority'. Similarly, politicians can often assume that their values *are* those of the majority, as Tony Blair may have been guilty of assuming in a Labour Party speech in 1995, two years before becoming Prime Minister:

> Socialism … is a moral purpose to life, a set of values, a belief in society, in co-operation, in achieving together what we cannot achieve alone. It is how I try to live my life, how you try to live yours – the simple truths – I am worth no more than anyone else, I am my brother's keeper, I will not walk by on the other side. We are not simply people set in isolation from one another, face to face with eternity, but members of the same family, same community, same human race. This is my socialism and the irony of all our long years in opposition is that those values are shared by the vast majority of the British people.

Blair assumes a normative value consensus that is 'shared by the vast majority of the British people'. It is debatable whether the majority shared all of Blair's values; however, the ideas expressed in this speech concerning family and community are vague enough for them to be hard to argue against. What Blair stated was not unique to socialism, nor indeed to New Labour. In the US Barak Obama, for example, has expressed similar sentiments, albeit with a dose of American individualism thrown in:

> If we Americans are individualistic at heart … it would be a mistake to assume that this is all we are. Our individualism has always been bound by a set of communal values, the glue upon which every healthy society depends. We value the imperatives of family and the cross-generational obligations that family implies. We value community, the neighborliness

that expresses itself through raising the barn or coaching the soccer team. We value patriotism and the obligations of citizenship, a sense of duty and sacrifice on behalf of the nation. We value faith in something bigger than ourselves ... And we value the constellation of behaviors that express our mutual regard for one another: honesty, fairness, humility, kindness, courtesy and compassion. (Obama, 2007: 55)

Similar to Blair, Obama was writing prior to becoming President. And like Blair, his argument was vague enough to be difficult to disagree with. He agrees with Blair that the values of family and community are most important, although he may not have agreed on the best ways of promoting family and community. Just as Blair states that he 'will not walk by on the other side', Obama emphasises a sense of empathy, which is 'at the heart of my moral code' (Obama, 2007: 66). For Obama, 'it is how I understand the Golden Rule[4] – not simply as a call to sympathy or charity, but as something more demanding, a call to stand in somebody else's shoes and see through their eyes' (2007: 66). The search for empathy is a theme to which I shall return later in this book. If Blair and Obama were right in that everyone agrees with some vague notion of family and community values, then what of anything more specific? Furthermore, who decides which values take precedence and the consequences for those who adhere to different values?

Who decides?

William David Ross (1930/2002) once proposed an axiological pluralism that there are several 'irreducible' things rather than just one intrinsic value. If people interpret goodness and badness differently it follows that there are plural conceptions of value. A fundamental question is who decides what is of value and what is valueless? With the quotes from Blair and Obama one can see how political capital can be an important determinant for what is generally seen as valuable. From a criminological perspective this power to dictate values has repercussions for criminalisation. For instance, if the political language centres on family and community values, threats to family and community – or at least particular conceptions of family and community – are more likely to be regarded as lacking value and may become criminalised. In Britain this was seen, for example, with New Labour's introduction of Parenting Orders with the 1998 Crime and Disorder Act, with parents facing censure because of the 'antisocial' exploits of their children

(Millie, 2009a). Returning to Howard Becker (1963), power lies with those he labelled as 'moral entrepreneurs', including politicians but also campaign and lobby groups, 'crusading reformers', industrialists, media campaigners and assumed 'experts' who all promote certain values by which we ought to live.

There are further individual and collective influences on what we value. For instance, a hedonist might value pleasure as intrinsically good, and if something leads to pleasure or makes pleasure more likely it might be regarded as extrinsically good. But what if this causes pain to others? The pleasure may be good for the hedonist but the consequences will not necessarily be good for anyone else. Furthermore, a masochist may take pleasure from pain, but is this necessarily 'good' for the individual or for society at large? For some people intrinsic goodness is found in knowledge or in the virtues of truth and justice; for others love is intrinsically good with extrinsic goodness placed on things or people that make love a possibility. A capitalist may find intrinsic value in wealth and anything or anyone who hinders the pursuit of money will be valueless (or certainly of less value). An artist or musician may find intrinsic value in beauty and see little value in money, in itself, beyond its extrinsic value for what it may lead to. From a criminological perspective a scholar interested in human rights might assert that anything that breaches a stated human right is intrinsically 'bad' and lacking value. Similarly, a critical criminologist interested in the 'view from below' might argue that social justice has intrinsic value and anything that makes social justice more likely is extrinsically good. For the zemiologist (for example Hillyard et al, 2004), harm is regarded as intrinsically 'bad', while anything that leads to harm will be extrinsically bad and could be criminalised. As noted in Chapter One, there are issues with who defines actions and omissions as harmful. 'Harm' is context dependent and socially constructed – the same as crime – by those with power. Notions of rights and social justice are similarly social constructions. There are questions over whose rights and justice take precedence.

There can also be exceptions for particular cases. For instance, a boxer will cause harm or pain, but this is usually with the recipient's consent and so the boxer will typically avoid censure – unless certain rules of boxing have been breached. During a period of state-sanctioned war a soldier may cause severe harm, pain and even death. Notwithstanding questions concerning the morality of war and killing – whatever the circumstances – the intrinsic badness of causing harm, pain and death will be viewed by some as an unfortunate cost of seeking 'the greater good', whatever that might be. Society has a set of rules ranging from the normative to the legal; yet there are exceptions to these rules and certain cases when rules can be bent or broken (Edgerton, 1985; Hinde, 2007). Of course, legal and normative rules can change so fundamentally that what is censured in one generation can be celebrated in the next – for instance the drinking of alcohol in the US during and post prohibition. The moral philosophy of rules and rule adherence is explored further in Chapter Six. What is important at this point is that the identification or perception of intrinsic and extrinsic goodness and badness has criminological effects, and these are influenced by individual and group value judgements. Those with greater political capital and power will have greatest influence in deciding what sort of values take precedence and where and when exceptions can be made.

Two value models

According to Ralph Barton Perry (1926/2007) something has value if people are interested in it. Conversely, something lacks value if it lacks interest. This is an appealingly simple proposition and in the criminological context something or someone who lacks sufficient interest will lack value and may be criminalised. Yet a plurality of interests means there would be conflict over whose interests – and thereby whose values – are superior. I may be interested in something that causes harm to someone else's interests. I may have multiple interests at different times and locations further adding to the confusion.

Interest is closely allied to desire and, according to James Griffin (1996), there are two models of value judgement that relate to desire. The first he labels the *perception* model, that something is desired because it is of value. We perceive something to be valuable and therefore desire it. Alternatively the second model is the *taste* model where something is valuable because it is desired, that value is reliant on personal and societal taste. The two are not mutually exclusive and there may be other models to add to the list. However, for criminology both are useful in trying to understand processes of criminalisation. Taste was something that concerned the Scottish philosopher David Hume, according to whom 'It is very natural for us to seek a *Standard of Taste*; a rule, by which the various sentiments of men may be reconciled; or at least, a decision afforded, confirming one sentiment, and condemning another' (1757: 207–8, emphasis in original).

Hume's emphasis on taste has most often been used to inform writings on aesthetics; yet it also applies to moral – and arguably criminal – concerns. The taste model dictates that, because we desire something, it has value. It is a model that has relevance to contemporary consumer capitalism; but, as Griffin (1996) has noted: '… what relevance have peoples' *actual* desires to what is in their *interest*? One of the discouraging facts of life is that one can get what one actually wants only to find that one is not better off, and sometimes even worse off' (1996: 21, emphasis in original).

It is not difficult to see how this model can have relevance to criminological concerns. At the simple level a thief may desire the social status that comes with possessions, thus giving them value to him, but not the means to gain them legitimately. A government may desire electoral victory, thus giving value to victory above other things of value, such as non-corrupt electoral practice.

The perception model is also useful in explaining certain criminological concerns. Here something is perceived to be valuable and therefore desired. For instance, I may perceive value in winning a race and therefore desire winning at all costs – including perhaps the use of banned substances. But as Griffin (1996: 22) attests, desires are not always rational – or at least they may not seem rational to the rest of us. He uses the example of a man intent on counting the blades of grass in a garden. The grass counter accepts that no one is interested and that the count is not useful in any way; yet he still desires to count grass and, therefore, to him it has some kind of value.

It seems that value judgements are tied in with people's perceptions, tastes and desires and that value is a qualitative concept with plural interpretations. Furthermore, different people confer different forms and degrees of value (see Lamont, 1955) to different things in different contexts. Conversely, and of relevance to criminology, people have different notions of what or who are valueless. Value judgements can be moral and aesthetic. In the next section I argue that they can also be prudential and economic. These four types of judgement are not mutually exclusive or discrete, yet work in such a way that leads to the criminalisation of certain actions or omissions, depending on context and who has the power to judge.

Four types of value judgement

Most decisions in life involve some sort of value judgement. What I argue here is that such judgements may involve any, or any combination of, moral, prudential, aesthetic or economic value judgements. I include here a simple example to illustrate this point (see also Millie, 2011). When considering whether to buy an expensive new shirt there is first an economic judgement. This can be as simple as whether I can afford it, or if the shirt is worth the asking price. Secondly, there is an aesthetic judgement on whether the shirt makes me look good. Next there is a prudential judgement concerning whether owning the shirt, or being seen wearing the shirt, will improve my quality of life. And lastly there may also be a moral judgement. For instance, is it right to spend so much on a shirt, or is the shirt made using exploitative methods or child labour? On the face of it buying a shirt is a simple decision; yet there may be a number of influencing value judgements to be made. If this is scaled up to more serious concerns – including whether to criminalise and if and when to punish – then the consideration of moral, aesthetic, prudential and economic influence becomes more serious.

Moral judgement

Moral judgements – and the impact of moral panics (for example Cohen, 1972) in particular – have been important criminological concerns for some time. Moral philosophy is considered in more detail in Chapter Three. There may be religious influence on what is regarded as good or bad, or perhaps majoritarian or utilitarian conceptions of right and wrong. Going with the view of the majority is superficially attractive, yet problems can occur if the majority hold prejudicial or discriminatory views. Moral 'rightness' can also be decided on humanitarian grounds, or based on issues of rights; but as noted, it is a question of who decides, and whose rights take precedence.

Aesthetic judgement

Over recent years criminology has shown growing interest in aesthetics, and especially in the significance of the visual with the emergence of visual criminology (for example Francis, 2009; Carrabine, 2012). According to Pierre Bourdieu (1979/1984), social snobbery dictates a progression of aesthetic taste from popular tastes, through middle-brow to assumed legitimate tastes. Of significance for criminology there can be criminalising consequences for what are regarded as illegitimate or sub-popular tastes (Millie, 2008). For instance, some forms of graffiti are criminalised, with the offender potentially facing a term in jail, while other more aesthetically acceptable forms, such as the use of stencils by Banksy and others, gain legitimacy and are celebrated widely. Aesthetic judgement is most often associated with such arts appreciation, although as explored in Chapter Four, there is also philosophical interest in everyday aesthetics (for example Saito, 2007) considering everyday objects, events and encounters. For instance a street drinker may be moved on for looking out of place (Cresswell, 1996), certain types of visible street protest are discouraged (Staeheli and Mitchell, 2008), and groups of loitering young people seen as a visible threat to urban civility (Millie, 2008). As is argued in Chapter Four, aesthetic expectations for particular locations and times can lead to censure for those that do not fit in. The example of a good view has previously been given. Aesthetic expectations dictate that the wrong type of people, or developments that detract from this view, may be criminalised and face banishment. As with moral judgements of value, context and the power to dictate aesthetic values are important.

Prudential judgement

According to James Griffin a further form of value judgement is prudential judgement, which concerns 'everything that makes a life good simply for the person living it' (1996: 19). Put simply, prudential judgements relate to issues of quality of life. Griffin admits that it is not possible to separate prudence from morals stating that 'We can neither understand morality independently of prudence, nor live well prudentially independently of living well morally' (1996: 68). That said, in order to understand value judgements and their relevance to criminology it is useful to see moral judgements and prudential judgements as at least partially separate. For instance, if someone's behaviour impacts on my quality of life then I am more likely to recommend censure, irrespective of whether this is the morally right thing to do. For Griffin prudence relates to issues of accomplishment, personal understanding, enjoyment, or 'deep personal relations' of friendship and love (1996: 30). Disapproval of actions or omissions is therefore due to their assumed negative impact on such 'quality-of-life' concerns. Within criminology quality-of-life concerns are particularly apparent in the areas of nuisance, antisocial behaviour and incivility. The Commissioner of New York Police, Bill Bratton (1995), in particular, has focused on what he labelled as 'quality-of-life crimes': 'namely street prostitution, low-level drug dealing, underage drinking, blaring car radios and a host of other quality-of-life crimes that contribute to a sense of disorder and danger on the street' (1995: 447–8). They are perceived as quality-of-life crimes for their assumed impact on what 'makes life good' for the rest of us (see Griffin, 1996: 19). In the UK such issues are recast as antisocial behaviours (Millie, 2009a) with those deemed to be antisocial often excluded and sometimes imprisoned. Judgements on who or what impedes quality of life can have very serious consequences.

Economic judgement

Economic judgements are important for everyday decisions (such as buying a new shirt); however in a capitalist society they can dominate all other considerations. This is the Marxist perspective, where entire classes of people can be criminalised if they hinder the capitalist machine. According to Steven Spitzer (1975: 642) such problem populations are identified by 'the threat and costs that they present to the social relations of production'. However, Marxists are not the only people to recognise the exclusionary and criminalising nature of capitalism. On a more mundane level, certain groups of young people, street drinkers or other loiterers have always been discouraged in shopping malls. If they are not there to spend they may be asked to move on. Furthermore, urban gentrification and regeneration can lead to exclusion, or what Neil Smith (1996) termed 'revanchism', with the urban poor – and perceivably more problematic populations – replaced by those with more spending power, the politically more powerful (and valued) middle classes (Millie, 2011). Economic judgements can also be made by governments when overlooking the crimes of large corporations, with a view that the valued economic contributions of such companies outweigh the benefits of litigation (see for example Whyte, 2009). Migration policy can also be dictated by economic judgements with exclusion for those who do not make the list of accepted migrants. As with moral, aesthetic and prudential value judgements, economic judgements of value can have serious consequences for those deemed to be less valuable or valueless.

Conclusions

This chapter has highlighted the centrality of values to criminological concerns: first that value-neutral research is not possible; and secondly, that value judgements are integral to understandings of good and bad, and what actions or omissions are celebrated, tolerated or censured. The chapter considered moral value judgements regarding good and bad, as well as deontic concerns of rightness, wrongness, obligation, requirement, reason for doing and what ought to be. Such moral concerns are explored in more detail in the following chapter. An important consideration here has been how to reconcile the multitude of moral values that exist within a pluralistic society. A purely relativistic position was discounted as this – in theory at least – could allow for behaviour that is generally regarded as intolerable, such as racism, rape, torture, slavery, paedophilia or genocide. The relativistic position would be that, while such activities are regarded as wrong in one society, somewhere with different moral or religious frameworks may take a different view. Instead, the view taken here is that there are some universal moral values that ought to be applicable to all and that some things are always wrong, no matter what the context – irrespective of whether local laws and customs suggest otherwise. Yet there is some interpretation and perception, and an important consideration is whose values take precedence. Politicians and other 'moral entrepreneurs' clearly have the power to dictate the values that characterise a particular society, whether or not influenced by majoritarian conceptions of value.

While an exploration of values may make for interesting academic discussion, the question is what relevance has this for criminological and criminal justice concerns? The main impact is on questions of criminalisation, or 'the processes by which actions or omissions become defined as crimes, or certain people or uses become defined as criminal or potentially criminal' (Millie, 2011: 278). According to Douglas Husak (2008) we live in a state of overcriminalisation, or what Antony Duff (2010) has called a crisis of criminalisation, where behaviours that are outside the norm or seen as too risky are too readily censured. It is the contention of this chapter that an understanding of values sheds light on why certain behaviours are criminalised and others are not, or are regarded as wrong in one situation but not in another. An understanding of moral values is clearly important here, but so too is an appreciation of how aesthetic, prudential and economic value judgements interact with moral judgements to determine which actions and omissions are celebrated, tolerated or censured. In the late-modern capitalist or neoliberal West economic values can dominate all other concerns. If something does not contribute to the economic worth of society, or does not make capital accumulation more likely, then it is deemed to have less value. Alternatively, one's impact on others' 'quality of life' can dictate perceived appropriateness – as exemplified by Bratton's (1995) interest in quality-of-life crimes. Taste also has an impact on behavioural acceptability – and if you do not contribute to an approved aesthetic then you may be moved on. The relevance of aesthetics to criminological questions is explored in Chapter Four. However, in the next chapter the importance of moral philosophy for criminology is considered in more detail.

Notes

[1] All Biblical quotes are taken from the New International Version.

[2] See also Luke 18:19.

[3] Popper does not deny the possibility that, while norms are man-made, they may have originated in religion.

[4] For more on the Golden Rule see Chapter Three.

THREE

Morality

Introduction

According to the British criminologist Anthony Bottoms (2002: 24), 'if they are true to their calling, all criminologists have to be interested in morality'. Moral philosophy, or ethics, is concerned with how we live and how we *ought* to live with one another. It considers what is good or bad, as well as deontic judgements of rightness, wrongness, obligation, requirement, reason for doing and what ought to be. Such concerns should be central criminological concerns. Criminologists assert that crime – or harm or deviancy – is a social construction and ask what it is about such actions (or inactions) that makes them unacceptable; in effect, what makes them good or bad, right or wrong. According to Hans Boutellier (2000) a criminal act tells us something of the morality of the offender and the morality of the society that defines this act as criminal: '... criminality is viewed as a moral problem and the moral significance of criminality occupies a central position. A criminal event is viewed as an incident whereby a person commits an act that has moral connotations because it is disapproved of, regardless of whether this is rightly so' (2000: 4).

In order to understand such criminalisation, criminology can therefore learn a great deal from closer engagement with moral philosophy; but similarly, moral philosophy can gain insight into moral censure from looking at criminology. As Boutellier has put it: 'Not only does every society get the criminality it deserves, to an even larger extent it gets the criminology it deserves. The way criminality is viewed nowadays can grant us some insight into the morality of our times' (2000: 4).

As was explored in the previous chapter, our values have a strong influence on what we regard as morally good or bad, what behaviour is to be celebrated, tolerated or censured as unacceptable. Also considered were relativist and universalist ethical positions. A relativist might claim that values and morals are down to personal opinion or taste, or just conventions that are culturally and context specific (see Driver, 2007). On the face of it relativism is attractive as it is seemingly tolerant of other ways of thinking and living. However, as noted, it can also be tolerant of actions and omissions that are generally regarded as morally *in*tolerant such as racism, slavery or rape. The conclusion to the previous chapter was that there are some universal moral truths that are – or perhaps ought to be – applicable to all. Yet beyond this there is room for some interpretation and individual and societal perception.

In this chapter three major approaches to understanding normative ethics are considered, these being virtue, consequentialist and deontological ethics. First, the relevance of virtue ethics to criminology is looked at, including the importance of character. This is followed by a more detailed exploration of consequentialist and deontological ethics. One way to consider ethical questions is to reflect on what it is that makes us want to do good and right, rather than bad and wrong. Within philosophy this is the domain of normative theories of obligation that ask what makes an act or omission right or wrong, and what makes us morally obliged to do right instead of wrong? In this chapter theories of obligation of relevance to criminology are considered, including consideration of social mores (customs and traditions), religious obligation, ethical egoism, and utilitarianism. Deontological perspectives such as social contract theory are also explored. The chapter then focuses on Immanuel Kant's work on the categorical imperative, the notion of universalisability, as well as Kant's focus on respect for persons (explored more fully in Chapter Seven). The chapter concludes by considering the 'Golden Rule' and its relevance to criminological concerns.

Virtue ethics and criminology

Virtue ethics are agent focused rather than act focused in that they focus on the qualities of the individual rather than the quality of a person's behaviour. A focus on virtues is not incompatible with moral theory based on actions or omissions; however, evaluation of behaviour is understood in terms of the character of the person. Consequentialist and deontological ethics focus more on behaviour and are considered next; but sticking with virtue ethics for now, this was the approach adopted by Aristotle in his Nicomachean ethics, his instructions on what was needed for a good and happy life. According to Aristotle a good person 'embodied all the excellences of human character' (Driver, 2007: 137). The key here is that good character is reflected in virtues such as honesty, justice, benevolence, courage, prudence, temperance and so on. Thus, an act is right 'if it exemplifies virtue, or if the virtuous person, the person who has all the virtues, would do it' (Bennett, 2015: 97). But just as no person is entirely 'good', there is no one that is entirely virtuous. Even within religion there are few examples of entirely virtuous people. Within Christianity, for example, Christ is the only entirely good and virtuous person – thus the popular phrase used by Christians when deliberating the 'right' choices in life: 'what would Jesus do?' Instead of looking for 'the virtuous person' it makes more sense to look for people who have character and provide examples of virtuous behaviour. Here there is a much longer list, including the likes of Martin Luther King, Ernest Shackleton, Mother Theresa, Mahatma Ghandi, and so on. While they may not have been perfect, they are exemplars of the virtues of courage, benevolence, justice and so on.

Yet, as with values, there is the question of who decides what is virtuous, or how behaviour is interpreted as being virtuous. For instance, temperance or self-control is often listed as a virtue, but restraint is not always seen as a good thing. Certainly, with regard to the drinking of alcohol, the abstinence preferred by the 19th- and early 20th-century temperance movement is not universally regarded as virtuous by late modern society. Another example is courage. The people listed above all showed great courage in their lives, from Martin Luther King's courage to stand up for what is right and just, through to Shackleton's courage that saw all his men saved after being stranded on the ice of Antarctica. There is also courage during wartime that is highly valued. Those who choose not to fight are viewed by some as cowards; but perhaps it is also courageous to say no, and choose not to fight. Conscientious objectors have faced imprisonment, or worse; but to stand up for your convictions and face the disapproval of your peers may be a very courageous thing to do. In a more obviously criminological context, a thief may show courage, but very few people would argue that this was a good thing. With this in mind, perhaps what are most important in determining which virtues are to be applauded are context and motive.

According to Aristotle virtues are the qualities that humans require for a 'higher' or 'flourishing' life. This can be criticised as being elitist, although there is perhaps nothing wrong with being aspirational. What might be wrong is to look down on those still trying to achieve. There is a further existential criticism of virtue ethics, stating that:

> ... there is no such thing as a pre-established pattern that dictates how human beings should live and what they should value. Human beings, the existentialists claim, are essentially free; they must set their own goals and aims; and

do not just 'find' what they ought to do written in the stars.
(Bennett, 2015: 98)

Despite such criticism, an appreciation of virtue ethics can be useful for criminology, in particular with regard to the formation of character needed to avoid or desist from criminality. For instance, according to Joanna Shapland and Anthony Bottoms (2011) a virtue ethics approach to desistance would recognise differences between someone's 'basic beliefs about themselves', that they are a good person and not an offender, and the probability that they may be tempted, 'led astray or otherwise commit an offence' (2011: 276). For Shapland and Bottoms 'it is not unreasonable to think of the path to desistance as gradually acquiring a set of more virtuous dispositions; of breaking old routines and habits of thought, and acquiring new ones' (2011: 276). Elsewhere Bottoms (2015) has compared desistance to the New Testament notion of repentance, translated from the Greek *metanoia*, meaning a change of mind or turning around. According to Bottoms, 'To achieve that kind of turnaround in their lives, people need first of all to decide to change; and such decisions are frequently motivated by a desire for a more positive future' (2015: 3). The desistor may be influenced by support from family and friends, and perhaps also from state and voluntary agencies, but to turn around also takes personal character. The need for character is not restricted to the offender; as Bottoms highlights, it may also be policy makers that need to turn around: 'Jesus's call to collective repentance does appropriately lead us to reflect on whether we need to "turn around" some of our policies in dealing with crime' (2015: 3).

Consequentialist and deontological ethics and criminology

While virtue ethics focus on the person, consequentialist and deontological ethics focus on the person's behaviour. It is to these that this chapter now turns. Put simply, a consequentialist normative theory of morality assumes that it is the consequences of action or thought that dictate rightness or wrongness. A classic consequentialist theory is utilitarianism, which is considered in more detail later in this chapter. A deontological normative theory judges the value of actions based on their faithfulness to prescribed rules or laws. As such deontological ethics are related to questions of duty or obligation and what ought to be. There are two main types of deontological obligation, these being societal and religious and these are considered next.

Societal and religious obligation to do the right thing

Each society has certain ways that most people do things, whether through tradition, habit or custom. For instance, most people would normally sleep in a bed, eat during the day and do not steal from others. According to William Graham Sumner (1906/1940) these are society's mores: 'The mores come down to us from the past. Each individual is born into them as he is born into the atmosphere, and he does not reflect on them, or criticise them any more than a baby analyzes the atmosphere before he begins to breathe it' (1906/1940: 76).

We are obliged by society's mores to behave in certain ways and this obligation is independent of personal inclinations; for instance, 'I ought to pay my debts, whether or not I feel so inclined' (Wellman, 1975: 30). The idea of having to follow society's mores is deontological; however, failure to comply with society's mores can have consequences of social stigma and maybe even criminalisation. As such it can also be regarded as a consequentialist idea. However, a clear disadvantage of using the mores as a basis for such theory is that each society will have its own version of the mores. For instance, Wellman uses the example of infanticide in some cultures once a family has reached a certain size: 'The theory that the mores make an act right or wrong implies that in some societies infanticide is right. But any reasonable person will recognize that this slaughter of helpless infants is morally wrong' (1975: 31).

As noted before, a relativist may not have difficulty with such a position; however, variety in mores across societies – and even within societies – means there is no possibility of objective truth. In short, by basing moral behaviour on social mores, just because this is how things have always been done, does not make them right.

Rather than being obligated by the mores, an alternative is an obligation to some kind of religious or spiritual law (as expressed variously in different religions but perhaps most explicitly in the Ten Commandments of the Old Testament). The problem with a religious basis for moral obligation is that not everyone is a believer. There is much to learn from religion regarding what ought and ought not to be done. For instance, the Ten Commandments have greatly influenced Western moral thinking and – of relevance to criminology – Western legal traditions. However, many do not believe in a deity and would object to a moral position that states we are all obligated to God. According to Boutellier (2000) Western culture may have once drawn on religion for moral and legal justification (specifically various strands of Christianity), but the secularisation and pluralisation that characterise post-modernity have meant religion's influence has diminished:

> ... the Code of Penal Law stipulates what is not allowed, but it does not say why. Up until the sixties, the explaining could be left to the various schools of religious thought ... the secularization process has since resulted in a fragmented morality, which is something very different from immorality. Nowadays the criminal justice system needs to substantiate the assumed general validity of its precepts to a conglomerate of multifarious moralities. (2000: 41)

If society's mores or religious laws do not obligate everyone to behave the same way, then perhaps it is a specific characteristic of the act that determines rightness or wrongness, or as WD Ross (1930/2002) has claimed, more than one characteristic of the act. Wellman summarises Ross's position thus: 'Each right-making characteristic makes an act prima facie right; each wrong-making characteristic makes an act prima facie wrong' (1975: 35). This takes us back to the arguments explored in the previous chapter concerning intrinsic and extrinsic value. The position in Chapter Two was that, while there is such a thing as extrinsic goodness, intrinsic goodness is harder to come by. Thus, an action or omission may be intrinsically 'good', but extrinsic consequences – such as impact on others – are more easily identified. In order to determine whether behaviour is good or bad one has to look at the impact on others. In criminological terms one can look at the impact on the victim, the offender or the wider human and environmental world. For instance, theft is wrong because of its negative impact on the victim. Theft may be intrinsically 'bad', but it is extrinsic harm to others that marks it out for societal censure. Illegal drug taking may be viewed as wrong due to the harmful impact on the person taking the drug as well as moral offence to wider society (Feinberg, 1985). The dumping of chemical waste may be an intrinsically bad thing to do, but is deemed harmful due to its extrinsic impact on the environment. This is a consequentialist view of morality, and it is to consequentialism that I turn to next.

Consequentialism

One way to consider the moral worth of actions or omission is to look at the consequences to the individual. This is ethical egoism where what makes something good or bad is its impact to one's self. For instance, I will pay taxes, not because it is the right thing to do in terms of paying one's debts or in benefiting wider society, but because non-payment will have a negative consequence for me in terms of feelings of guilt or, if caught and convicted, in terms of criminal record, sentence and shame. From this perspective the self-interested thing is the morally right thing to do. Much of sentencing theory is based on this premise, especially theories of specific and general deterrence (see for example Ashworth et al, 2009) that assume the self-interest of avoiding severe penalty will deter one from committing crime. However, as a basis for moral obligation this form of consequentialism is unsustainable. Self-interest can also be selfish or prejudiced. In terms of criminal justice it could also justify corrupt practice and inhuman treatment (Banks, 2015: 27).

Hobbes' social contract

In *Leviathan* (1651/1990) Thomas Hobbes adopted a pessimistic view that each of us is self-interested and therefore unable to cooperate – unless of course it is demonstrated that it is in our self-interest to do so. Thus, according to Christopher Bennett (2015: 131), Hobbes saw that 'moral rules are those that it is in each person's interest to obey' because the consequences of not adhering to these rules, to live outside of society, is a 'war of all against all':

> Whatsoever therefore is consequent to a time of war, where every man is enemy to every man; the same is consequent to the time, wherein men live without other security, than what their own strength, and their own invention shall furnish them withal. In such condition, there is no place for industry; because the fruit thereof is uncertain: and consequently no culture of the earth; no navigation, nor use of the commodities that may be imported by sea; no commodious building; no instruments of moving, and removing, such things as require much force; no knowledge of the face of the earth; no account of time; no arts; no letters; no society; and which is worst of all, continual fear, and danger of violent death; and the life of man, solitary, poor, nasty, brutish, and short. (Hobbes, 1651/1990: 465)

To avoid such a fate a social contract is deemed necessary consisting of various rules for social living; but this also has the self-interested benefit of social cooperation. It is a deontological perspective where following a set of rules is our duty – but also to our benefit. Rules (including social contracts) are explored in much more detail in Chapter Six. The social contract is also consequentialist, emphasising the consequences to the self and to society of not adhering to a set of rules.

Utilitarianism

Hobbes's ideas influenced the utilitarianism that followed, in particular the work of Jeremy Bentham and John Stuart Mill. Utilitarianism emphasises the maximisation of happiness in society. Bentham's utilitarianism was a version of 'act utilitarianism' where, at its simplest, if an action has more happy consequences, rather than unhappy consequences, then it is morally acceptable. According to Bennett (2015: 56) an advantage of such utilitarianism is its compatibility with naturalism in that we do not need to appeal to a higher power in order to understand what is valuable. The emphasis on consequences and happiness makes utilitarianism a consequentialist and hedonistic philosophy. While consequentialism and hedonism may be 'as old as human thought itself' (Baumgardt, 1952: 35), it was Jeremy Bentham who gave utilitarianism its identity. Unlike ethical egoism, which focuses on the consequences to the individual, utilitarianism considers the consequences to all persons, or all sentient beings; as JJC Smart (1973) neatly summarises: '... the only reason for performing action A rather than an alternative action B is that doing A will make mankind (or, perhaps, all sentient beings) happier than will doing B' (1973: 30).

The utilitarian regards pleasure or happiness as having intrinsic value, whereas pain or unhappiness have intrinsic disvalue. As previously noted, the problem with such a simple assessment of the value of pleasure and pain is that some people take pleasure in pain, and some take pleasure in activities that most would see as lacking in value. Yet Bentham did not see particular pleasures as more or less valuable than others. Thus, an 'everyday' pleasure has the same value as experiencing high art; as Bentham famously put it:

> The utility of all these arts and sciences, – I speak both of those of amusement and curiosity, – the value which they possess, is exactly in proportion to the pleasure they yield. Every other species of pre-eminence which may be attempted to be established among them is altogether fanciful. Prejudice apart, the game of push-pin is of equal value with the arts and sciences of music and poetry. If the

game of push-pin furnish more pleasure, it is more valuable than either. (Bentham, 1825: 206)

According to Bentham, while different pleasures have the same value, the size or quantity of pleasure could be measured in terms of intensity, duration, ferocity, purity, certainty, and so on.

Bentham's egalitarianism has been criticised, not least by John Stuart Mill who distinguished between high and low pleasures with higher pleasures having greater quality, if not necessarily quantity. Mill's perspective was a version of 'rule utilitarianism' where an act is right if it adheres to certain rules that lead to greatest pleasure or the greatest good. However, separating what are high and low pleasures can be simply a matter of taste. The problems that come with trying to create hierarchies of taste are explored in Chapter Four on aesthetics. Of significance to criminology, claims of higher and lower pleasures can have criminalising consequences, with certain low pleasures more likely to be deemed unacceptable. Similarly, having 'unacceptable' tastes may lead to censure. A further relevance to criminology is that utilitarianism assumes that the maximum pleasure or good can be calculated. Certain strands of positivist criminology – especially crime science – have embraced the techniques of cost-benefit analysis. It is assumed that the costs of a particular crime control or prevention technique, or perhaps a rehabilitation programme, can be set against the benefits in order to calculate maximum utility to society.

An alternative version of utilitarianism was proposed in the 20th century by Karl Popper (1945) who, rather than focusing on the maximisation of happiness, considered the minimising of suffering to be of greater value:

> ... all moral urgency has its basis in the urgency of suffering or pain. It is, I believe, the greatest mistake of utilitarianism (and other forms of hedonism) that it does not recognize that from the moral point of view suffering and happiness must not be treated as symmetrical; that is to say, the promotion of happiness is in any case much less urgent than the rendering of help to those who suffer, and the attempt to prevent suffering. (1945: 205, note 6)

For Smart (1973) this could be seen as a 'negative utilitarianism'. Popper himself called it 'humanitarian and equalitarian ethics' (1945: 205, note 6).

Criminology has had a turbulent relationship with utilitarianism. For some, the post-war mainstream in criminology, which has been dominated by positivism, has had too close a relationship with the state (for example Taylor et al, 1973). In Britain, for example, many criminologists – myself included – have worked with or for the Home Office. A form of utilitarianism is adopted where the maximum utility is often defined by the state, as are the crimes to be controlled. During the 1970s this status quo in Britain was critiqued by a group of critical criminologists who formed the National Deviancy Conference in 'a clear attempt to develop an "anti-utilitarian" criminology that was able to conceptualise, theorise and research crime and deviance from outside the State's agenda of crime control' (O'Brien and Penna, 2007: 248). Yet, critical criminology is also largely utilitarian, albeit a utilitarianism that does not rely on the state to define what is harmful to society. Drawing heavily from Marxism, the state itself is regarded as causing greatest harms. The utilitarianism of critical criminology has more in common with the humanitarian and equalitarian ethics proposed by Popper. In his book 'Against Criminology', Stanley Cohen (1998) makes a similar point, that *all* criminology is dominated by utilitarian thinking:

> Criminological theory in every form from classicism through to positivism and its critics has been dominated by utilitarian thinking. The justification for intervention – whether punishment, treatment, or whatever – is in terms of the supposed ends to be achieved. Marxism is also utilitarian in this ordinary sense of the relationship between means and ends, but in addition proposes a special type of 'consequentialism' in which the ends justify the means because the end *must* follow. (1998: 29–30, emphasis in original)

Cohen contrasts this utilitarianism with an abolitionist criminology (1998: 30). According to Willem De Haan (2003: 381) abolitionism 'is based on the moral conviction that social life should not and, in fact, cannot be regulated effectively by criminal law and that, therefore, the role of the criminal justice system should be drastically reduced'. For Cohen, abolitionism is an absolutist rather than utilitarian theory in that abolitionists would 'not support undesirable policies only because they may lead to desirable ends'. This may or may not be true always; but Cohen has highlighted an important criticism of utilitarianism – and of consequentialism more broadly – that ends *should not* always justify the means. To illustrate this point Cohen quotes Emma Goldman on the Russian revolution: 'No revolution can ever succeed as a factor of liberation unless the means used to further it be identical in spirit and tendency with the purposes to be achieved' (Goldman, 1925: 261).

In a utilitarian context, if the benefit to society being sought is the maximisation of happiness, then the unhappiness of a minority might be an acceptable cost. Of course, this would not be the opinion of the victims of revolution, or similarly in a criminological context those disproportionately targeted by crime control measures or who are more often incarcerated. In both the US and UK (and elsewhere) this is most likely to be poor and minority ethnic populations (for example Bowling and Phillips, 2007; Loury et al, 2008). In Australia it may be disproportionate policing of indigenous communities (Cunneen and Tauri, 2016). Racial profiling and targeted stop-and-search procedures have been justified on a simple ends-justifying-the-means basis. However, it is morally dubious to give preferential value to some members of society (the majority) over others (those targeted). This is a limitation of majoritarian political philosophy that gives preference to the views of the majority, and is especially problematic when the majority hold prejudicial or stereotypical views of minorities.

To give a further example from personal experience, I once spoke at a Home Office seminar on crime reduction where a team of researchers from a different institution claimed that publicity about burglary reduction efforts had a measurable impact on the level of crime. This is not surprising. If a potential burglar saw that the police were putting extra resources into reducing burglary in a particular area then they may change their offending behaviour to different times, locations or even to other forms of acquisitive crime for the duration of the police effort. However, during the seminar the researchers went further, claiming that if publicity can reduce crime then the police do not necessarily have to do anything at all (they just need to say that they are doing something). At the time I was not convinced and suggested there may be ethical implications of such an approach. The team's findings were later published in the American journal *Criminology and Public Policy*, where they proposed the use of 'phantom' crime prevention schemes: 'This would simply involve the advertising of "phantom" crime prevention schemes that do not exist. Furthermore, informal networks could be used to create rumors of police clampdowns or heightened police activity. This deception does have moral implications, but it has the potential for very cost-effective crime reduction' (Johnson and Bowers, 2003: 518).

From a purely utilitarian, cost-benefit perspective, the end may justify the means where the end is a simple numerical reduction in burglary within a given area. However, the authors were right to acknowledge possible moral consequences of deception. If burglary is a morally wrong thing to do, then using another moral wrong (deceit) might also be unjustifiable. According to JL Mackie (1977) this is an issue of universalisability; that the same view should be taken about similar moral actions:

> Moral judgements are universalizable. Anyone who says, meaning it, that a certain action (or person, or state of affairs, etc.) is morally right or wrong, good or bad, ought or ought not to be done (or imitated, or pursued, etc.) is thereby committed to taking the same view about any other relevantly similar action (etc.). This principle, in some sense, is beyond dispute. But there is room for discussion about how it is to be interpreted, about its own status, and about what then follows about the content and the status of morality. (Mackie, 1977: 83)

People are not consistent and may well contradict a moral judgement made in one context when making moral judgements elsewhere, even if this is in a similar situation. However, from this perspective deception in crime prevention would be morally wrong. Similarly, and perhaps more seriously, racial profiling or stop-and-searching one ethnic group and not another would also be morally wrong. The notion of universalisability draws on Immanuel Kant's categorical imperative and it is to this that I now turn.

Kant's categorical imperative

Immanuel Kant's philosophy is deontological in that he proposed various a priori[1] rules for moral living. His work is non-consequentialist, instead focusing on whether actions conform to a 'moral law', his categorical imperative. This was explored in his *Grounding for the Metaphysics of Morals* (1785/1990) in which Kant articulated various formulae for absolute or categorical laws for moral reasoning. The first is his Formula of Universal Law (FUL):

> Act only according to that maxim whereby you can at the same time will that it should become a universal law. (1785/1990: 1031)

Kant also suggested a variant, his Formula of the Law of Nature (FLN):

> Act as if the maxim of your action were to become through your will a universal law of nature. (1785/1990: 1031)

Kant's ideas fit with Mackie's universalisability. So, for example, suppose someone lives by a maxim to steal from others, this person should question whether this could become a universal law. The answer is clearly that it could not as it would mean the thief would be happy for others to steal from him. The converse maxim 'I shall not steal from others' could be universally applied and becomes a categorical moral imperative. One example given by Kant related to borrowing money knowing that it could not be repaid:

> The maxim of his action would then be expressed as follows: when I believe myself to be in need of money, I will borrow money and promise to pay it back, although I know that I can never do so. Now this principle of self-love or personal advantage may perhaps be quite compatible with one's entire future welfare, but the question is now whether it is right. I then transform the requirement of self-love into a universal law and put the question thus: how would things stand if my maxim were to become a universal law? He then sees at once that such a maxim could never hold as a universal law. (Kant, 1785/1990: 1032)

For students of law and criminology this is a useful way of understanding why certain actions or omissions should be seen as morally wrong and may be criminalised. It is also a useful heuristic for understanding what might be wrong with the law, or why certain actions should never be censured. In the above example of borrowing money there are clear benefits to the individual in taking the money, but this would put the benefits they accrue above the costs to the lender (and to other future borrowers who will no doubt end up paying higher interest rates). This prioritisation of the self over others is expressed in Kant's second formula, his Formula of Humanity as End in Itself (FHE):

> Act in such a way that you treat humanity, whether in your own person or in the person of another, always at the same time as an end and never simply as a means. (1785/1990: 1036)

The borrower and the thief clearly treat the lender/victim as a means to an end. Kant gave a further example of the moral wrongness of suicide, with a person using their own humanity as a means to an end: 'If he destroys himself in order to escape from a difficult situation, then he is making use of his person merely as a means so as to maintain a tolerable condition till the end of his life' (1785/1990: 1036). Contemporary criminal law in most Western countries does not take such a dim view of suicide, although it is an act that is frequently regarded as a moral wrong. Of importance is Kant's emphasis on the need for respect for self and for other persons. This respect is explored in more detail in Chapter Seven. Kant's emphasis on absolute moral laws has overlaps with religious views on morality. In fact his view on humans as ends and not means has a lot in common with the Biblical instruction to 'love your neighbour as yourself' (Mark 12:31). This emphasises the importance of both loving the other (the neighbour) and of loving the self. In Kant's terms, neither the neighbour nor the self are means to an end.

The Golden Rule

The categorical imperative has been compared to what has been termed the 'Golden Rule', a maxim that has existed in numerous cultures and religions, including the works of Plato and Aristotle, through to Buddhism, Zoroastrianism and Stoicism (see Hertzler, 1934). It is most famously expressed by Jesus in the Sermon on the Mount:

> So in everything, do to others what you would have them do to you, for this sums up the Law and the Prophets. (Matthew 7:12)[2]

In Brahmanism (in the Upanishads) the Golden Rule is expressed thus:

> Let no man do to another that which would be repugnant to himself; this is the sum of righteousness … a man obtains the proper rule by regarding the case as like his own. (cited in Hertzler, 1934: 420)

Like the categorical imperative the Rule is universal. It is also reciprocal in that you must treat others in a way that you would expect them to treat you. According to Joyce Hertzler (1934) the Rule is popular as an aid to social control, but it is not coercive nor dictatorial, unlike other forms of social control, such as mores, laws and public opinion;

instead: 'The Golden Rule … operates from within the individual, and results in the voluntary limitation of behavior. It is control that is subjective, self-initiatory, and self-coercive, but which redounds to social benefit, due to the uniqueness of its psychology' (1934: 428).

In short, the Golden Rule is centred on the individual, 'but it is not individualistic' (1934: 439). The benefits of adherence to the Golden Rule are for the self and for wider society. The Rule's relevance to criminology is in its impact on behaviour. Returning to the earlier examples of stop and search and racial profiling, if the police do not want people to be disrespected, then they should not be disrespectful of groups often regarded as 'police property' (Cray, 1972; Reiner, 1992). Similarly with the example of 'phantom' crime prevention schemes, if the police and wider society do not want to be treated dishonestly, then they should not use dishonest methods in crime prevention. This basic idea can be transferred to all sorts of criminal justice situations. For instance, in this use of custody, prisoners would be treated in a way that one would hope to be treated oneself. Of course, people have differing expectations and beliefs that would impact on this idea. I may think the idea of being in prison is abhorrent and so would call for the abolition of the prison system. Someone else may think it entirely fair to be imprisoned if they have done wrong, and so it would also be fair for others. Thus the Golden Rule is a subjective and individualistic approach to morality, but one with wider societal impacts.

For Paul Ricoeur (1990) the Golden Rule has potential problems, especially as expressed within Christianity. For instance, there is a possible connection between the Golden Rule's reciprocity and the Old Testament *jus talionis*, or rule of retaliation as expressed in Exodus 21:23–25: 'But if there is serious injury, you are to take life for life, eye for eye, tooth for tooth, hand for hand, foot for foot, burn for burn, wound for wound, bruise for bruise.'

According to Ricoeur (1990) the notion of an eye for an eye is retaliatory and limited, and as such, an improvement – albeit a limited improvement – on simple vengeance, which can be limitless. However, the Golden Rule is different to retaliation and of greater moral value as it anticipatory rather than reactive. Yet, for Ricoeur (1990) the reciprocity of the Golden Rule may still be problematic. For instance, according to Jesus:

> If you love those who love you, what credit is that to you? Even sinners love those who love them. And if you do good to those who are good to you, what credit is that to you? Even sinners do that. And if you lend to those from

whom you expect repayment, what credit is that to you? Even sinners lend to sinners, expecting to be repaid in full. But love your enemies, do good to them, and lend to them without expecting to get anything back. Then your reward will be great, and you will be children of the Most High, because he is kind to the ungrateful and wicked. Be merciful, just as your Father is merciful. (Luke 6:32–36)

Ricoeur calls this the Christian 'economy of gift and its logic of superabundance' (1990: 395). This 'superabundance' or generosity is because God has been generous with us, and so we should go and do likewise (1990). This does not deny the logic of the Golden Rule, but reinterprets it. However, it is possible that this generosity was the intention of the Golden Rule all along, that to 'do to others what you would have them do to you' means treating others with love and mercy *even if* you do not expect it in return. It is an attitude to life, or a challenge to expectations, that could be adopted by those who do not believe in God as much as by those who do. It may at least lead to improvements in interpersonal moral behaviour. This superabundance is also reflected in the instruction to turn the other cheek (Matthew 5:39). It can be summed up by the imperative to love your enemy: 'You have heard that it was said, "Love your neighbour and hate your enemy." But I tell you, love your enemies and pray for those who persecute you' (Matthew 5:43–44).

This would be a major challenge to criminology. A criminal justice system based on the logic of superabundance and love for the enemy would need to be generous, merciful and loving. It would need to be characterised by grace, the art of giving without expecting in return. It is an idea I return to in Chapter Seven on the subject of respect.

Conclusions

Many of the day-to-day interests of criminology are clearly moral concerns, whether to criminalise, how to police, consideration of the limits of social control, when and how to punish, and whether and how to side with the powerless. What this chapter has demonstrated is that there is much crossover between moral philosophy and criminology. Various approaches to moral questions have been considered, from a focus on virtues, through to theories of obligation and various consequentialist and deontological ethical approaches. The importance of character was highlighted, along with the limitations of ethical egoism and utilitarianism. Criminology has a close relationship with utilitarian thought, yet the National Deviancy Conference of the 1970s attempted to create an anti-utilitarian criminology. As highlighted, Stanley Cohen (1998) was of the view that all criminology is dominated by a concern with maximising utility in terms of the ends justifying the means. However, as Cohen notes, the ends do not always justify the means; an important point when considering, for example, the limits of social control, methods of investigation, the process of justice, use of torture or methods of punishment. Furthermore, there are issues when maximum utility is defined by the state. Even majoritarian conceptions of utility can be problematic. By definition, a concern with maximising the utility for the majority means that concerns for a minority are lessened. If criminology is on the side of the oppressed, the downtrodden, the 'other', then utilitarian theory becomes less attractive.

An alternative approach to understanding morality is the Golden Rule, or Kant's interpretation in the categorical imperative. Unlike utilitarianism, Kant's approach is non-consequentialist and instead focuses on whether actions conform to a 'moral law'. His Formula of Universal Law (FUL) is a useful place for criminologists to start in order to understand why certain actions or omissions ought to be regarded as morally wrong and, maybe, censurable; to 'Act only according to that maxim whereby you can at the same time will that it should become a universal law' (1785/1990: 1031). Thus, the powerless should not be mistreated or disproportionately policed as this action could not become a universal law. In other words, the person or agency doing the mistreating or over-policing would not will that they themselves would be the victim of such disproportionate action. Moreover, any action or omission that regards others as a means to an end is unjust. The examples given in this chapter were theft and borrowing knowing that you could not repay, but across the spectrum of criminology there are many other examples. So the death penalty is morally wrong as it treats the person on death row as a means to an end – this being retribution or an assumed – although misconceived – deterrence effect. At the other end of the spectrum, various crowd control techniques become morally questionable as the liberty of the protestor is a means to other public order benefits. The subjectivity of what constitutes a means and an end needs to be acknowledged. And both the categorical imperative and Golden Rule are individualistic understandings of morality, although they have wider societal impacts. However, such a focus would be a major challenge for criminal justice agencies. Perhaps an even more radical challenge to ideas of criminal justice, as well as to criminology, would be the Christian economy of gift and logic of superabundance (Ricoeur, 1990), to treat others with love and mercy, even if you do not expect it in return; although as Ricoeur notes, this was perhaps the intention of the Golden Rule all along.

Notes

[1]   Knowledge independent of experience.

[2]   The Golden Rule is usually positively stated; however it is also expressed in the negative, for instance in Confucianism it is stated: 'What I do not wish men to do to me, I also wish not to do to men' (Hertzler, 1934: 160).

FOUR

Aesthetics and crime

Introduction

There is a picnic bench on the shore of Loch Morlich in Scotland with a panoramic view of the wild Cairngorm mountains, one of the most beautiful views that I know. I may even go so far as to say that the landscape is sublime. But when I say the view is beautiful or sublime, what do I mean? Similarly, what makes something stand out as good art, or what characteristics make an everyday object or encounter a beautiful contribution to contemporary life? These are the concerns of aesthetics. In this chapter the relevance of aesthetics to criminology is explored. However, back in the Cairngorms, what if I discover that the apparent wilderness landscape is an illusion; that much of what I see is manmade, being formed by centuries of grazing, shooting and forestry management? In more recent years the skiing industry has scarred the mountainside with runs, lifts and a mountain railway. Does this have an impact on the area's 'wild' aesthetic? Globally, pure wilderness is increasingly rare and, in the British Isles at least, it is arguably no longer evident.[1] In the UK many of the most 'wild' landscapes are legally regulated as National Parks (including the Cairngorms). According to Joe Hermer (2002: 69), North American National Parks sell a wilderness aesthetic that is regulated as highly ordered: 'a landscape where the "wild" qualities of "nature" are manufactured by the promotion of quietness, decency and hygiene'. This type of aesthetic regulation makes landscape something that could be of interest to criminologists.

For me 'natural' or 'wild' beauty are not necessarily dependent on there being no human impact; however, when describing the English landscape the author DH Lawrence had a less favourable view of man's impact on the countryside: 'The real tragedy of England, as I see it, is the tragedy of ugliness. The country is so lovely: the man-made England is so vile' (1929/1977: 389). Lawrence was mistaken in making a distinct split between the countryside and 'man-made' spaces. A lot of people consider the country to be a rural idyll (Halfacree, 1996), without necessarily realising that the rural is often only possible *because* of human influence – and part of this influence is in terms of aesthetic regulation. With the advent of National Parks the same is also true for many of the wilder places on the planet.

This chapter considers the relevance of aesthetics to criminology. People's expectations of what is aesthetically acceptable, appropriate or tolerable are considered, as well as criminalising consequences for people or things that interfere with a preferred aesthetic. The law is used to prevent certain kinds of activities due to aesthetic considerations; yet some activities that are broadly perceived as aesthetically detrimental may still be permitted due to other considerations, including the power of the applicant. Various examples are given.

According to John J. Costonis (1989: 1), 'Aesthetics and law are an odd couple'. Considerations range from the mundane through to major development issues. For instance, on the shore of Loch Morlich, if I turn my gaze and discover that where I am sitting has become a dumping ground for litter or that someone has graffiti-ed the bench I am sitting on, these are both aesthetic *and* criminological considerations. At the other extreme, if I discover plans to use the land for military exercises, for a golf course or wind farm, should there be criminalising consequences for spoiling my view? I consider the view of the Cairngorms to be beautiful, but admittedly this beauty comes, in part, from association as I proposed to my wife at this spot. Aesthetics is also concerned with such emotional affect and this chapter concludes by considering the relevance of emotion to an aesthetic criminology.

Aesthetics is often narrowly conceived as a philosophy of arts or landscape appreciation; yet it is much broader than this, being concerned with our emotional and sensory experience of the world around us, including how we judge beauty in whatever form. It is focused on perception and representation and, as such, is often portrayed as a poor relation to other more 'solid' areas of philosophy – as Elisabeth Schellenkens (2007: 1) has noted: 'Philosophical Aesthetics is a discipline with fewer natural friends than foes'. Clive Cazeaux (2011) acknowledges that aesthetics is traditionally on the margins but that greater understanding of the interconnectedness of subjectivity and reality has led to a shift where aesthetics is 'vital to an understanding of the relationship between human being and the world' (2011: xi).

Each of us has an idea of what is beautiful depending on taste (a theme this chapter returns to), including perhaps notions of what makes a beautiful view, beautiful art, people, morals, lifestyles, or even perhaps a beautiful profit. The chapter looks at, for example, celebrity graffiti writers, hoodie-wearing youths and Gypsy, Roma and Traveller communities regarded as 'spoiling' majority conceptions of beauty in urban and rural landscapes. Take for example a group of hoodie-wearing young people who are often regarded as an unacceptable presence on the street due to a perception that they are intimidating and a threat to others' use of public space. There may be reputational reasons for this based on previous experiences of young people, or how young people are portrayed in the media. There may also be aesthetic reasons in terms of the language of fashion, young people's mannerisms and choice of language. Yet in different contexts the same young people may not be intimidating at all. In an earlier study (Millie et al, 2005), different respondents recounted how an acquaintance had seen a group of young people and crossed the road to avoid them, only to realise the group contained the acquaintance's own son. Whether the story is true or an urban myth, 'freely used to illustrate the unfounded fears of older people' (2005: 25), it highlights the potential for aesthetic cues to inform perception of threat. In this chapter examples are given when such cues can lead to criminalisation.

Aesthetic judgements are first considered in terms of arts and landscape appreciation. The distinction between conceptions of objective and subjective beauty are then examined. In line with Kantian aesthetics it is contended that beauty is entirely subjective. Of relevance to criminology, the subjectivity of aesthetic judgements has repercussions for the criminalisation of people or things perceived as unattractive. Taste is clearly important in determining acceptability; but so too is power to define what is aesthetically tolerable. Both taste and power are considered in more detail. Power in particular is looked at with regard to acceptability or censure within rural and urban landscapes. The role of semiotics is also considered. The chapter concludes by considering the scope for an aesthetic criminology.

Aesthetic judgements in art and landscape

In the opening chapter to this book the example was used of a urinal – attributed to Marcel Duchamp – that was submitted to an art exhibition. According to Cabanne (1997: 115) Duchamp had demonstrated that 'anything could be "art", which meant, in its turn, that art could be any old thing'. In effect the artist had concluded that if he says it is art, it is art. This may be the position of much modern and contemporary art today; yet in art criticism there is also consideration of what constitutes 'good' art. The quality of art is a classic concern for aesthetic philosophy, alongside the aesthetic experience and the possibility of objective beauty. The British artist David Hockney once stated: 'Always live in the ugliest house on the street – then you don't have to look at it' (Artists and Illustrators, 2013). There is clearly humour in what he was saying, but also a hint at Hockney's view on beauty. Put simply, it is much nicer to look at beautiful things than ugly things. For a recent series of paintings Hockney focused on the everyday Yorkshire landscape in Britain, the kind of things you see from the car window: the embankment by the side of the road, a group of trees, a hedge. One of Hockney's influences is Edward Hopper (Aldred, 1995) who had previously done the same for the urban and rural American landscape; he stopped to look at the everyday and turned it into something beautiful. This chapter takes the view that people will have different perspectives of what is beautiful. For instance, Hockney's paintings may include some of my favourite images; yet you may not value them at all. Beauty is therefore subjective – although it is acknowledged that this view is not universally held. Another British artist, Damian Hirst, has more of an existential fascination with death, with beauty being apparent in the transitory nature of existence. Hirst is famous for his butterfly pictures, skulls and pickled sheep. According to Hirst (see Havlin, 2010): 'butterfly or skull, flower or animal carcass ... I don't think there is much difference in the end'. Hockney and Hirst have two quite different ideas of beauty; but the important point is that one is not necessarily more valid than the other.

Aesthetics is not only concerned with what is conceived as 'high art', but also with what Yuriko Saito (2007) has termed everyday aesthetics. Saito was influenced by Henri Lefebvre's (2000) ideas on 'everyday life', what Philip Wander (2000: vii) describes as the 'dull routine, the ongoing go-to-work, pay-the-bills, homeward trudge of daily existence' (see also de Certeau, 1984). According to Saito (2007: 9) aesthetic concerns ought to include 'any reaction we form toward the sensuous and/or design qualities of any object, phenomenon, or activity'. Thus, everyday aesthetics may concern the feel of a woolly cardigan, an appreciation of the repeating pattern of a parquet floor, a fascination with the shape of a tree, or perhaps the reading of graffiti carved into the glass window of a train.

In terms of graffiti and street art, probably the most famous contemporary exponent is Banksy. His view on graffiti is as follows: 'Some people become cops because they want to make the world a better place. Some people become vandals because they want to make the world a better *looking* place' (Banksy, 2006: 8, emphasis in original).

In Banksy's statement there is conflict between what he sees as beauty, as a valid contribution to urban life, and what the law says he is doing, which is something quite illegal, be it labelled as criminal damage or antisocial behaviour. For the criminologist a focus on aesthetics may seem trivial; yet graffiti artists that lack Banksy's celebrity status have ended up in prison for doing exactly the same thing. It seems aesthetic judgement on what is acceptable or unacceptable (street) art can have serious consequences (Millie, 2008). According to Germaine Greer:

> Nearly all graffiti are just annoying, but you have to put up with the millions of naff ones if you want the occasional brilliant one. … [We could be] giving the defacers marks out of 10, to remind the artists that there are people out there who have eyes to see, and as much right to say what they think as the artists. The work then becomes a palimpsest, a dialogue between artists and public. Most tags deserve the single-word comment 'prat'. (Greer, 2007)

Despite the contention that anything can be art, all artistic expression attracts aesthetic judgement; and according to Greer, a score out of 10 would help to distinguish between 'naff' and brilliant graffiti. The problem with such a perspective is that it is dependent on taste. Put simply, who is to determine what is 'naff' and what is brilliant? And can aesthetic worth ever be rationally calculated and given a score? If the general view is that the art is 'naff', should the artist be arrested? To make judgements on the value of graffiti and street art − where bad art is criminalised and good art celebrated − adds an element of jeopardy to the occupation of graffiti writer or street artist (Millie, 2008). This chapter is interested in who are making such judgements in terms of power and context, and why certain tastes are prioritised; but, taking Greer's contention that graffiti can be given a score out of 10, the objectivity versus subjectivity of beauty is considered next.

Objective versus subjective beauty

Just as Germaine Greer considered giving graffiti a score out of 10, towards the end of the 18th century William Gilpin considered criteria for classifying landscapes (for example 1789; 1792). Gilpin's classifications were based on whether a landscape was suitable for a painting − whether it was picturesque. (Sixty years later John Ruskin (1857) also used picturesque criteria to categorise architecture.) Gilpin assumed that landscape beauty could be rationally and objectively classified and favoured the romantic image of the countryside; the craggy rock, the ruined castle or abbey semi-enveloped by nature. He was critical of the type of naturalistic gardens favoured by Lancelot 'Capability' Brown (on whom more later). While Brown's gardens were beautiful, for Gilpin, at least, they were not picturesque (Turner, 2013). His suggested 'improvements' were to:

> Turn the lawn into a piece of broken ground: plant rugged oaks instead of flowering shrubs: break the edges of the walk: give it the rudeness of a road: mark it with wheel tracks; and scatter around a few stones, and brushwood; in a word, instead of making the whole *smooth*, make it *rough*; and you make it also picturesque. (Gilpin, 1792: 8, emphasis in original)

His 'improvements' were not limited to gardens. For instance, on visiting Tintern Abbey in the Wye Valley, Gilpin thought the Abbey ruin *almost* perfectly adhered to his ideal for the picturesque. To make it perfect he famously suggested 'a mallet judiciously used' (1789: 47). In a later publication Gilpin went further in describing how Palladian architecture could be turned from being elegant and highly pleasing into something having picturesque beauty:

> A piece of Palladian architecture may be elegant in the last degree. The proportion of its parts – the propriety of it's [*sic*] ornaments – and the symmetry of the whole, may be highly pleasing. But if we introduce it in a picture, it immediately becomes a formal object, and ceases to please. Should we wish to give it picturesque beauty, we must use the mallet, instead of the chisel: we must beat down one half of it, deface the other, and throw the multitude members around in heaps. In short, from a smooth building we must turn it into a rough ruin. (Gilpin, 1792: 7–8)

At the time it was a popular view. For instance, Jane Austen made reference to Gilpin's picturesque in *Pride and Prejudice* (1813/2003) and *Northanger Abbey* (1817/1995). From a contemporary pluralistic perspective Gilpin's view may seem nonsense as there are multiple standpoints on what is aesthetically pleasing. Furthermore, it could be regarded as an incitement to criminal damage.

Over the years aesthetic judgement (alongside economic judgement) has led to the destruction of seemingly beautiful buildings in what Colin Ward (1973) and Dan Cruickshank (1973) have called the vandalism of planners and developers. An example used by Cruickshank was the 1962 destruction of a neo-classical arch outside Euston railway station in London, 'an example of incredible philistinism on the part of authority with power, in the face of informed, but powerless, individuals' (1973: 189). The arch did not fit with the modernist aesthetic promoted by the new Euston station. It is possible that planners and developers have caused more damage to cityscapes than more conventionally identified vandals. After the rediscovery of a large proportion of the stone from the Euston Arch, at the time of writing, Cruickshank is campaigning for its reinstatement.[2] This chapter returns to issues of power in dictating aesthetics; but what the Euston Arch example demonstrates is the subjectivity of aesthetics, with developers and campaigners having quite different opinions. This chapter take a view that Gilpin was essentially wrong in claiming that aesthetic beauty can be rationally calculated.

Kantian aesthetics

Although Gilpin emphasised rational, objective classification, writing around the same time Immanuel Kant held the view that aesthetic taste is subjective, that 'an objective principle of taste is impossible' (1790/2011: 12). Kant's view was that there are no objectively beautiful or sublime landscapes, or works of art, or anything else. Instead, our assessments on aesthetic worth are dependent on taste. To give an example, Kant considered the beauty of a flower:

> To say, This flower is beautiful, is tantamount to a mere repetition of the flower's own claim to everyone's liking. The agreeableness of its smell, on the one hand, gives it no claim whatsoever: its smell delights one person, it makes another dizzy ... beauty is not a property of the flower itself. For a judgment of taste consists precisely in this, that it calls a thing beautiful only by virtue of the characteristics in which it adapts itself to the way we apprehend it. (Kant, 1790/2011: 10)

Thus, something is beautiful because we perceive it as beautiful, and not because there is some inherent calculable quality in the object, flower, view or person that makes it beautiful. It pleases us, and this pleasure will be different for different people. Aesthetic considerations are often restricted to the visual and aural. For the flower there is also smell. Other senses can be added to this aesthetic appreciation. For criminological analysis this is an important observation. Over recent years there has been growth in what has been labelled visual criminology, involving a critical engagement with the image of crime (for example Carrabine, 2012; Young, 2014). Alison Young has considered the scope for a criminological aesthetics that considers meaning derived 'from the affective nature of the spectator's encounter with the image' (2014: 161). By broadening focus from the visual to include all the senses then perhaps an aesthetic criminology is possible (Millie, 2016). This is an idea considered in the conclusions to this chapter.

In writing about 'legal aesthetics' in US planning and land use law, John J. Costonis (1989: 15) has claimed that 'Aesthetics considerations are ubiquitous'. They are also subjective and this subjectivity makes planning and land use law all the more difficult; yet for Costonis, aesthetics is not the only subjective consideration:

> Lawmakers therefore must attend to these [aesthetic] considerations unless they are prepared to shut down land use regulation in its entirety. To suppose, moreover, that the other values advanced by land use controls are hard, coherent, objective, nonmanipulable, and fully accessible to economics or any other form of analysis is to substitute one kind of tooth fairy logic for another. (Costonis, 1989: 15)

It is true that aesthetics is not the only consideration, and that it is not the only subjective factor in land use law – or for that matter in criminal or other forms of law. In Chapter Two aesthetic judgements were set alongside other moral, economic and prudential considerations. All such value judgements are subjective. The importance for criminology is that all have an impact on what we regard as acceptable, tolerable or censurable behaviour. The key determinate for all such judgements – but perhaps especially for aesthetic judgement – is taste.

The importance of taste

Gilpin's criteria for a picturesque landscape and Greer's scorecard for graffiti are both examples of taste dictating what is regarded as aesthetically praiseworthy. But does it make sense to claim to have better taste than someone else? Should majority tastes dominate? And if not, whose tastes are most important? According to the conservative philosopher Roger Scruton (2009), for example, aesthetic tastes matter:

> In a democratic culture people are inclined to believe that it is presumptuous to claim to have better taste than your neighbour. By doing so you are implicitly denying his right to be the thing that he is. You like Bach, she likes U2 ... she likes Jane Austen, you like Danielle Steel. Each of you

exists in his own enclosed aesthetic world, and so long as neither harms the other, and each says good morning over the fence, there is nothing further to be said. ... [But] your neighbour fills her garden with kitsch mermaids and Disneyland gnomes, polluting the view from your window. ... Now her taste has ceased to be a private matter and inflicted itself on the public realm. (2009: 133–4)

Someone else's tastes may cause you harm. For instance, it is conceivable that living next to a garden full of gnomes could cause you psychological distress, or perhaps living next to someone who plays their U2 too loudly may adversely affect your quality of life (see also Millie, 2014b; 2016). But to claim to have better tastes than someone else is patronising; as the philosopher Carolyn Korsmeyer (2005: 275) has suggested: 'Those who conceive of themselves as having good taste may condescend to those with "inferior" tastes, while the later may consider the former mere snobs.' Furthermore, having 'poor' taste may in effect be criminalised. For instance, in England and Wales the 2003 Anti-Social Behaviour Act (s 66) stipulates the unacceptability of having a high hedge if it causes:

'so much of a barrier to light or access as (a) is formed wholly or predominantly by a line of two or more evergreens; and (b) rises to a height of more than two metres above ground level'.

A taste for tall hedges (and privacy) is legislated against if it adversely impacts a neighbour's access to his property or access to sunlight. It may also affect property prices (Millie, 2014b). Pierre Bourdieu (1979/1984) once charted a social aristocracy of culture, from popular, through middle-brow to legitimate tastes. Those with legitimate tastes were the ruling classes – as measured by cultural capital, educational attainment and occupation. Jeff Ferrell (1996) has termed this an aesthetics of authority with the powerless labelled as having 'popular' or 'illegitimate' tastes. The importance of power is considered next.

The importance of power

In the 19th century Napoleon III instructed Georges Haussmann to restructure Paris. The city was growing rapidly and the existing medieval street pattern was struggling to cope. The chosen solution was to open up the city with a number of wide boulevards that cut though the existing arrangement. The buildings along the boulevards were to have a unified form and style and today give Paris its unique look and feel. While aesthetics was clearly important to the design, it has been argued that the wide boulevards also made it more difficult for revolutionaries to construct barricades. Correspondingly, it was easier and quicker for troops to get to any uprising (see for example Mumford, 1961). In this example aesthetic considerations and the power to suppress go hand in hand.

Haussmann's Paris was the backdrop to Charles Baudelaire's poem 'The Eyes of the Poor'. The ruling class's aesthetic judgement of the visibly poor is reflected in the experiences of a wealthy couple visiting one of the new cafés on a Haussmann boulevard. The story is retold by Marshall Berman (1982: 149):

> As the lovers sit gazing happily into each other's eyes, suddenly they are confronted with other people's eyes. A poor family dressed in rags – a graybearded father, a young son, and a baby – come to stop directly in front of them and gaze raptly at the bright new world that is just inside .... He is 'touched by this family of eyes' .... 'I turned my eyes to look into yours dear love, to read my thoughts there' ... she says, 'These people with their great saucer eyes are unbearable! Can't you tell the manager to get them away from here?' (1982: 149)

The sight of 'a poor family dressed in rags' was deemed to be out of place (Cresswell, 1996) and the suggested solution was simply to 'get them away from here', to banish (Beckett and Herbert, 2010). Those with power are seen attempting to dictate an acceptable urban aesthetic at the expense of the powerless. It is a situation that has resonance today. In the UK, for example, Dispersal Orders have been used to move on those thought likely to be antisocial (Crawford and Lister, 2007; Millie, 2009a). Introduced with the 2003 Anti-Social Behaviour Act, the Orders were controversial as they censured both behaviour and presence. They were applied to a designated area in circumstances:

> That any members of the public have been intimidated, harassed, alarmed or distressed as a result of the presence or behaviour of groups of two or more persons in public places in any locality in his police area (the 'relevant locality'), and that anti-social behaviour is a significant and persistent problem in the relevant locality. (s 30(1)(a) and (b))

Legislating against certain unwanted behaviours may be sensible; yet there are clear risks of stereotyping once legislation starts to talk in terms of a person's 'presence' causing 'harassment, alarm or distress'. Those perceived as a threat to an acceptable aesthetic are most likely to be dispersed: the visibly indigent, the street drinker, the youth wearing certain 'problem' fashions, the street sex worker.

As noted, those with supposedly inferior tastes are often condescended to, and these include the youth wearing the fashion of trainers and hoodie – read as potentially problematic, possible gang member or just a young person up to no good. In the UK it has been the fashion of the 'chav' (Hayward and Yar, 2006) or 'ned' (Brown, 2008). For instance, in 2005 Kent's Bluewater shopping centre banned the wearing of hoodies (Hayward and Yar, 2006; Millie, 2009a). The aim was so that everyone's face could be seen by CCTV; yet the move also reinforced the view that hoodie-wearing youths are problematic. This was despite the same hoodies being on sale within the centre. The sensibilities of the more powerful – shopping and spending – public took precedence.

A further example is the censure of fashion which appears offensive. Joel Feinberg once observed that 'Because of legislators' tendency to overreact to offensiveness we should approach the subject with great caution' (1985: 5). An example from the UK was the arrest in the early 2000s of members of the pro-hunting campaign group the Countryside Alliance for wearing t-shirts with the words 'Bollocks to Blair' across them. At the time the multinational clothing company French Connection was unhindered in selling equally offensive clothing with the logo FCUK (see Millie, 2009a). The criminalisation of fashion is not new. For instance, in the UK the 1723 Black Act criminalised having your face blackened or being otherwise disguised (Treadwell, 2008). In Victorian Britain, dressing in certain fashions of the urban poor could get you mistaken for a 'hooligan' or 'peaky blinder' and a target for police action (Pearson, 2009).

The result of priority being given to an aesthetic preferred by the more powerful (and in late-modern neoliberal democracies the powerful are those that can spend) is that the powerless are more likely to be banished from view; a situation that Beckett and Herbert (2010: 8) have described in the US:

> Increasing swathes of urban space are delimited as zones of exclusion from which the undesirable are banned. The uniformed police are marshaled to enforce and often delineate these boundaries; they use their powers to

monitor and arrest in an attempt to clear the streets of those considered unsightly or 'disorderly'.

So far, consideration of aesthetics and power has focused on the visibility – or otherwise – of unwanted populations on the street. According to Michel Foucault a relationship between aesthetics and power extends to other areas of criminological interest. In particular, in Foucault's work on crime and punishment he drew attention to the 'spectacle of the scaffold' (1977: 32) and the broader 'theatrical apparatus' of penal justice (1977: 282). According to Foucault, there was an overlap of criminality between 'those who enforced the law and those who violated it' (1977: 283) in that the punishment meted out was also inherently criminal. One of Foucault's examples was the 19th-century French criminal, Lacenaire. Prior to Lacenaire's execution the bourgeoisie, in effect, turned him into what today would be a celebrity. Here Foucault hinted at the possibility of an 'aesthetics of crime' as an 'art of the privileged classes' (1977: 284). The idea of an 'art of the privileged' is key to understanding relationships between aesthetics, power and criminology. With the demise of the scaffold Foucault talked of the removal of the public from the immediate spectacle of punishment. However, by distancing the public, representation became all the more important (Brown, 2006). The spectacle in effect remained, but it was the privileged classes, those with power, that dictated how the rest of us experienced crime, criminals and punishment – be it through popular fiction, the printed press or through TV drama (Cheliotis, 2010). This may be broadly true today, although recent history has seen a massive change in our media diet with the expansion of the internet and the rise of citizen journalism (Greer and McLaughlin, 2010). The aesthetics of crime that we experience is no longer solely that dictated by the privileged, although powerful media and political elites clearly still dominate.

Power and context are key determinants for what is deemed aesthetically acceptable and appropriate behaviour. Examples have included the banishment of the unsightly, the spectacle of punishment and the representation of crime and criminals. A further example is regarding landscape aesthetics to which I now turn. Examples are given from the 18th century through to today. Power has clearly been key in determining which landscapes are regarded as aesthetically 'right', and which activities are detrimental to an acceptable landscape aesthetic and therefore criminalised.

Power and landscape aesthetics

Throughout the 18th century Enlightenment views on what constituted a beautiful, picturesque or sublime landscape were developing. As noted, in Britain Lancelot 'Capability' Brown (1716–83) was busy creating vast landscape parks for the land-owning classes. He preferred a new naturalism – in preference to pre-existing formal gardens – where gardens and whole estates were reshaped to create idealised, yet apparently 'natural', settings for country houses. Woods were planted, lakes created, follies built and hills removed to create the perfect vista. If villages got in the way they were simply moved:

> Brown didn't rearrange landscapes; he completely demolished them and started again. It was quite on the cards for him to move villages, as he did at Milton Abbas ... At Chatsworth he moved the village of Edensor and removed a hill which had a much better long-distance view behind it. (Titchmarsh, 2003)

The tastes of the powerful resulted in spectacular landscape parks, many of which are still with us today. However, what is of most relevance to the current text is the impact on those who had to make way for such developments. They were regarded as not contributing to the aesthetic being sought and were moved out of sight. If criminology is interested in social harm and social justice, then it ought to be interested in such impacts of landscape taste. In the 18th and 19th centuries more dramatic events were taking place in Scotland with the Highland and Lowland Clearances, with tenant farmers evicted en masse to make way for sheep farming. Many of the evictions were unpleasant. For instance, in describing the Highland evictions following the potato famine of the 1850s, Tom Devine (1989: 163) claims that 'Several involved "compulsory" emigration; others were carried out with great brutality'. The sheep farming has since largely been replaced by shooting estates; and some of these have been replaced by National Parks. While aesthetic concerns may not always have been central to the clearances, the tastes of the powerful had a powerful impact on the powerless – as well as a dramatic impact on the landscape.

Similar processes occur today. For instance Gypsies, Roma and Travellers are often 'moved on', evicted or persuaded to settle in designated areas as their presence does not comply with a planned-for rural idyll (Halfacree, 1996). To give a high-profile British example, a large group of travellers was evicted from a site at Dale Farm in Essex in 2011. Different agencies worked together to make the eviction possible, resulting in 'over 100 police officers in full riot gear, using public order policing methods, including the use of Tasers, [who] forced entry to unauthorised development in order to facilitate private bailiffs to carry out the eviction for the local authority' (James, 2015: 224). The travellers' crime was to build their site without planning permission and on designated 'greenbelt' land. An integral part of planning law is consideration of aesthetics and, it seems, in this instance the travellers did not fit what was expected for the greenbelt. In North America aesthetic concerns are similarly expressed in planning and development law through zoning rules and ordinances or through National Park regulations with only certain forms of development permitted in specified zones. This is not to say that aesthetic controls are necessarily a bad thing. The creation of National Parks, listing of historic properties, creation of greenbelt and conservation areas, or the architectural design review process are examples where a lot of good can result from aesthetic consideration of planning issues. Yet, there may also be harm, especially if the tastes of the powerful are seen to dominate.

Another example from Scotland is Donald Trump's recently opened golf course on the Aberdeenshire coast. According to Trump, 'I have never seen such an unspoiled and dramatic sea side landscape and the location makes it perfect for our development'.[3] Not only was it 'unspoilt', but it also had protection as a Site of Special Scientific Interest (SSSI). Despite local opposition and initially being turned down by local planning, the course was approved by the Scottish government and opened in 2012. Trump's next move was to go for expansion with a hotel and leisure complex. According to criminologist Hazel Croall (2016) the impartiality of the police in this case has been called into question:

> Particularly controversial was what was seen as a 'land grab' by the Trump organisation in 2010, when a fence was erected on the land of a prominent campaigner: an incident observed by police officers who, despite being shown the resident's title deeds, maintained that the organisation had the right to act in this way. (2016: 140)

In criminological terms what was occurring could be described as both a corporate and environmental crime. It seems, just as in 18th-century Britain, power can dictate whose landscape/development preferences takes precedence. In 2015 Trump took the Scottish government to the UK Supreme Court over their approval for a planned wind farm offshore from his golf course. Trump was not happy as he thought the wind farm would spoil the view for his golfers, saying – apparently without any irony – that former First Minister of Scotland Alex Salmond 'should be ashamed of himself because he is ruining one of the great landscapes in the world' (see Tovey, 2015). It is quite possible that Trump's development had already caused more than enough damage. On 16 December 2015 Donald Trump lost this particular legal challenge.[4]

These examples demonstrate how power and context are important determinates for aesthetic acceptability and possible criminalisation. Included in Chapter Two was consideration of moral, prudential and economic judgements alongside aesthetic judgements. In the Dale Farm example, aesthetic and prudential concerns (regarding the quality of life of those not within the traveller camp) appeared more important than moral issues. In the Trump example economic and aesthetic interests dominated with priority seemingly given to economic concerns regarding inward investment and attracting tourists. In all examples the judgements of those with less power were frequently less important.

Aesthetic power and the urban landscape

Issues of power, image and aesthetics come into play in dictating urban as well as rural landscapes, especially in terms of the management of public and semi-public spaces. According to Sharon Zukin (1995: 7): 'The look and feel of cities reflect decisions about what – and who – should be visible and what should not, on concepts of order and disorder, and on uses of aesthetic power.'

As noted, the result can be the banishment from the street of homeless people, street sex workers, young people and other categories of 'them' that are deemed to be aesthetically inappropriate. A case in point is a recent retail development in Liverpool in the UK named 'Liverpool One'. According to the development's publicity it is 'bringing some of the biggest names in retail together in one beautiful shopping arcade' (undated). Here perceived beauty comes at the cost of excluding certain 'others', such as street drinkers, that are deemed inappropriate as they detract from a neoliberal shopping aesthetic. In fact, there is an acceptable aesthetic for street drinking, where city workers drinking outside a pub are acceptable, but a street drinker on a bench is not (Millie, 2008). Context and power are clearly important. At Liverpool One CCTV and private security guards are utilised to move people on and ensure that those who remain are there to spend. It is a commercial decision, but also an aesthetic choice regarding how to maintain the right image for the development. This is not a uniquely British phenomenon (Mitchell, 2001; Beckett and Herbert, 2010; Millie, 2016), but again hints at the importance of aesthetics and taste, and the possible criminalising consequences for those deemed unacceptable.

Aesthetics and semiotics

The presence of street homeless people, groups of young people – or in fact anyone – sends a signal to be perceived by others. This may be interpreted as potential threat, someone to be ignored, tolerated or welcomed. Semiotics is a useful way of interpreting such signals (for example Barthes, 1972; Eco, 1979) and is an idea developed by Martin Innes and colleagues in their signal crime perspective (for example Innes and Fielding, 2002). The idea of signal crimes was also influenced by the psychology of Paul Slovic (1992), according to whom all risk-related events have a 'signal value', which reflects 'the perception that the event provides new information about the likelihood of similar or more destructive future mishaps' (1992: 124; see also Millie, 2014a). According to Innes and Fielding (2002) the police have the potential to be read as reassuring and as signals of control (Millie and Herrington, 2005). In fact, a semiotic iconography for the police has evolved involving the uniform, police car, (usually) the colour blue and the chequerboard motif. In the UK it also includes the blue lamp. All of these aspects are there to be read as signs of reassurance (Millie, 2012). But, of course, a person's interpretation of the police is not solely dependent on aesthetic cues. Other issues of misconduct or disproportionate policing methods may have more of an impact.

A structuralist interpretation of such signs and signals is that all readers interpret them the same way (for example Barthes, 1972). Alternatively, an interpretivist view is that 'individuals are creative agents that make their own meanings' (Millie, 2012: 1094; see also Millie, 2014b). This is the understanding of semiotics adopted here, where aesthetic experiences, including encounters with others, can mean different things to different people. The language of semiotics is not only useful for understanding interpersonal relations, but also people's experiences of art and architecture – including the architecture of the criminal justice system. Thus a prison might be 'read' as 'brutal, bland or beautiful' (Jewkes and Moran, 2014) or a police station might be regarded as an intimidating fortress, a secret place, or somewhere where the public is welcomed (Millie, 2012).

Conclusions: an aesthetic criminology

This chapter has considered the relevance of aesthetics to criminology and examples have been given where aesthetic considerations have led to criminalisation. The aesthetic tastes and preferences of those with power have tended to dominate, often leading to further marginalisation of the powerless. Thus, shopping centre managers can dictate the right sort of customers, a large golf course gets approval on a designated SSSI, and Gypsies, Roma and Travellers are moved on as they are deemed to be inappropriate. From a criminological perspective – and in line with Yuriko Saito (2007) – everyday aesthetic experiences are just as important as more traditional high art aesthetics. For example, the aesthetics of street drinking was highlighted, with the drinking habits of office workers encouraged, while at the same time drinking by 'street-life people' (see Moore, 2008) actively discouraged. In terms of everyday art appreciation, the wrong sort of graffiti or street art that is not perceived to be good enough is criminalised, with the possibility of censure for the graffiti writer or artist. Conversely, the right sort of graffiti that is in the right place, or street art by 'celebrity' artists such as Banksy, are celebrated as valued contributions to urban life, attractors of tourists, and contributors to urban regeneration.

Despite claims that an objective measure of beauty is conceivable (for example Gilpin, 1789; 1792; Greer, 2007), the chapter has contended that tastes are subjective. This is in line with a Kantian conception of taste, that 'an objective principle of taste is impossible' (1790/2011: 12). Thus, something is beautiful or aesthetically pleasing because we perceive it as such. Yet, those with power can dictate 'approved' tastes, with people or things that interfere with these tastes either criminalised or banished. This was true for the villagers who got in the way of 'Capability' Brown's plans in the 18th century. It is also true today for powerless groups deemed to be unsightly. What these examples have hopefully demonstrated is that aesthetic concerns can also be criminological.

As noted, recent years have seen expansion in what has been termed visual criminology. While important work is being conducted under this umbrella term, it is possible that a focus on the visual could be broadened to an aesthetic criminology that considers all the senses (Millie, 2016). For instance, Mariana Valverde (2012: 77) has noted how municipal law can 'actively regulate taste and culture … by banning certain sights and sounds and smells but also … by using law to compel people to maintain aesthetic standards'. An aesthetic criminology would be concerned with such regulation of tastes.

Aesthetic criminology would also be interested in emotion and our affective responses to sensory encounters. Semiotics is a useful way of understanding how such encounters are read. In terms of affect, the urban geographer Nigel Thrift (2004) has highlighted that 'Cities may be seen as rolling maelstroms of affect. Particular affects such as anger, fear, happiness and joy are continually on the boil, rising here, subsiding there' (2004: 57). An aesthetic criminology would be interested in such emotive and affective responses. Earlier in this chapter the example of the view of the Cairngorm mountains from Loch Morlich was used, a view made all the more special for me as this is where I proposed to my wife. Such love of place (Bachelard, 1969) has been labelled by Yi-Fu Tuan as 'topophilia' (1974), or 'An affective bond between people and place or setting' (1974: 4). An aesthetic criminology would consider how such bonds are defined, altered or broken by experiences of crime, deviance or social harm, or conversely by experiences of social control and the criminal justice system.

Aesthetic criminology might also be interested in those who subvert our aesthetic expectations of place by promoting alternative ways of seeing and living. This might include various urban interventionists, including work by 'traditional' artists, but in a public setting, as well as work of graffiti writers and street artists, flash mobbers, impromptu street performers, guerrilla gardeners, guerrilla knitters and other urban activist and artistic groups (see for example Brejzek, 2010; Brisman, 2010; Millie, 2016). According to Kim Prusse (1999: 9) urban interventions are, mostly, '… not advertised. They are not in gallery settings, not signed by artists, not for sale, and do not have arrows pointing to them screaming "this is art!"'. Such activities would be of interest to the aesthetic criminologist as they clearly challenge aesthetic norms and the regulation of taste. They frequently also use illegal 'beautification' methods to promote their own vision of urban living. Furthermore, they challenge notions of acceptable order and disorder, themes that are developed in the following chapter.

Notes

[1]   For instance, Oliver Rackham (1990) has argued that there is no wildwood left in the British Isles.

[2]   See the work of the Euston Arch Trust: www.eustonarch.org.

[3]   See www.trumpgolfscotland.com.

[4]   *Trump International Golf Club Scotland Limited and another (Appellants) v The Scottish Ministers (Respondents) (Scotland)* available at: www.supremecourt.uk/cases/docs/uksc-2015-0160-judgment.pdf.

FIVE

Order and disorder

Introduction

In 2002 an episode of *The Simpsons* was broadcast in which Bart Simpson had an infectious illness forcing him to live in a clear plastic bubble. In one scene Bart was told off for slurping his soup. Bart's reply was a simple, "My bubble, my rules". His response neatly encapsulated the ethical egoism of late modern individualism, where the self is supreme and often blind to its impact on others. According to Michael Hechter and Christine Horne (2009) the basic problem of social order is how this individualism can be reconciled with the necessities of living a social existence:

> The problem arises because human beings are both individual and social. If we were each living alone on a private planet, we could do whatever we wanted and would never have to worry about anyone else. … Every individual inhabits a separate physical body and thus each has his or her own emotions, information, feelings, and ambitions. Yet we are not completely independent. (2009: 1)

Individualism – or a lack of regard for others – means it is okay for a single-occupancy car to be parked in a parent and child parking zone because you are just popping into the supermarket; or to push in front of someone queuing for a cinema ticket because you really must see the film; or to take someone's car without permission because it is raining and you don't want to get wet. My bubble, my rules, and to hell with the consequences for anyone else. Yet, if everyone is motivated entirely by self-interest then social order is impossible to achieve. According to Hechter and Horne (2009: 1), for social order to be possible, '[p]eople must be able to coordinate their actions and they must cooperate to attain common goals'; as the journalist Lynne Truss once observed, 'all the important rules surely boil down to one: *remember you are with other people; show some consideration*' (2005: 12, emphasis in original).[1] The former UK Prime Minister Margaret Thatcher once famously declared:

... you know, there's no such thing as society. There are individual men and women and there are families. And no government can do anything except through people, and people must look after themselves first. It is our duty to look after ourselves and then, also, to look after our neighbours. (in *Woman's Own* magazine, 1987, cited in *The Guardian*, 2013)

It is the argument of this chapter that Thatcher was wrong. Yes, people must look after themselves, but for there to be any prospect of social order this cannot be in preference to looking after our neighbours; as noted in Chapter Three, this is in line with Jesus's famous instruction in the Gospel of Mark (12:31) to 'Love your neighbour as yourself'. Of course, not every reader will be convinced by religious instruction; yet, as a general rule equal love for neighbour and self is a good place to start when considering the possibility of social order.

Criminology's interest in social order is in the impact of disorder, the mechanisms created to make order more likely, and the consequences for those being ordered. It is also in the meaning of order and disorder and the sometimes fluid boundaries between the two. Some form of social order is clearly beneficial in order for societies to operate; however it can also have malign impact when married to the social control of people or things regarded as being disorderly, or of a lower social order. Intrinsic to social order are issues of normativity, power, class and deference, and corresponding challenges to the status quo, all of which interest the criminologist.

The classification of behaviours as crimes, and the policing of such 'crimes' are clear ordering devices which separate people into law abiders and law breakers. Criminology itself is not immune to such ordering and divides people between respectable 'us' and deviant or harmful 'others'. Whether the others are members of deviant youth sub-cultures, governments or international conglomerates, it is easy to categorise and separate ourselves from those who do harm to us. The reality is that all of us are rule breakers to varying degrees – whether breakers of legal, moral or normative rules concerning crime, deviancy and harm. In terms of legal rules, during the 1970s Jason Ditton (1977) and Stuart Henry (1978) drew attention to the everyday law breaking of fiddling, pilfering, fare evasion and dealing in stolen goods, which, in many contexts, are normalised practice. As Henry observed:

... with the unveiling of the hidden economy we can see that clear-cut divisions between right and wrong are dissolved. We discover that everyone, from dustmen to doctors and from directors to dockers, is on the fiddle. ... if we are *honest* we can see that dishonesty is, to a greater or lesser extent, something we are all guilty of. (1978: 172, emphasis in original)

Contemporary examples of everyday law breaking include motorway speeding (Wells, 2012), making false insurance claims (Karstedt and Farrall, 2006), unauthorised parking in a disabled bay (Chenery et al, 1999) and minor fraud in order to get a child into a preferred school (Millie, 2008). In the UK the parliamentary expenses scandals of 2009–10 proved that Members of Parliament are just as likely as the rest of us to be everyday law breakers. More recently in 2015 the international scandal that enveloped Volkswagen over 'cheats' to emission tests and dubious CO_2 figures demonstrated how multinational corporations also find ways to break the rules.

Even if rules are not broken, then they are clearly there to be bent; and there are always exceptions to rules that can be found (Edgerton, 1985; Hinde, 2007). Such rules are explored in more detail in Chapter Six. If everyone is bending or breaking the rules of contemporary living, then how is social order maintained? Furthermore, is community possible with the individualism that comes with late modernity? This is the focus of this chapter, which considers the conflicts between individualism and the need to live with others. How order can be maintained is also considered. The importance and limits of social order are discussed, drawing particularly on work on anomie and postmodern perspectives on catastrophe and chaos. The chapter also looks at various demands for an aesthetic order to where we live; but first we consider anomie and chaos.

Anomie and chaos

As previously highlighted in Chapter Three, there are certain mores, religious or cultural obligations, normative values and legal rules that dictate what is generally regarded as morally acceptable. In the 19th century the French sociologist and philosopher, Émile Durkheim (1893/2014) considered situations when people's ideas and values change. Durkheim is famous for his thinking on anomie, or normlessness, a situation in society when normative standards and values are breaking down. During periods of anomie social bonds are broken, new ways of living become evident, and society struggles to come to grips with the new while attempting to hold on to the past.

A clear example was during the Industrial Revolution when normative and legal rules of society lagged behind social and economic change. Here anomie was evident during a period of economic progress; however, according to Durkheim, it is also likely during periods of economic downturn. The result is an increased challenge to society's norms and greater crime and disorder while society adjusts to the new reality. The recent economic downturn may have cast doubts over some of Durkheim's assertions, with crime rates in many Western countries falling despite expectations – although there are also doubts over the reliability of some crime figures and a great deal of 'new' crime facilitated by the internet that has gone unrecorded. Be that as it may, Durkheim's views have had an exceptionally strong influence on criminology and sociology, most notably on the work of Robert Merton (1938) on social strain to achieve the goals set by society – which could be achieved by legitimate and illegitimate means. For both Durkheim and Merton crime and anomie are 'normal'. However, what is defined as 'crime' may change as society changes; as the criminologist Leon Radzinowicz (1966: 74) has put it: 'Crime may change its shape as society itself changes, but it remains a part of all societies'.

Anomie is a challenge to the existing order and in that regard can be relabelled as disorder. Durkheim's and Merton's work highlights that such disorder is not necessarily a bad thing as it allows society to reconfigure to a new social and economic reality. In fact, Durkheim went further, suggesting that not only is crime normal, it is necessary for society to function and change. According to Radzinowicz: 'To abolish crime completely it would be necessary to have a penal system so stringent that it would exclude all deviation on the part of individuals. Without deviation there could be no adaptation, no change, no progress; a society could not survive' (Radzinowicz, 1966: 72–3).

Of course, many people would not be receptive to the suggestion that crime is normal and even beneficial to society, especially those who have suffered as victims of crime. Nonetheless, the important point here is that understandings change regarding what is normal, criminal, or ordered and disordered. Furthermore, some disorder, or even 'a certain anarchy' (see Sennett, 1970: 108), may even be good for society. This is an idea that this chapter returns to.

Postmodern perspectives

Postmodern perspectives have taken an emphasis on anomie and disorder forward by drawing on catastrophe and chaos theories in mathematics (for example Lyotard, 1984). Catastrophe theory emphasises breakdown and collapse as integral to the evolution and development of systems. According to the mathematician René Thom (1975: 1, cited in Sim, 2011) the physical world is composed of 'the ceaseless creation, evolution and destruction of forms'. As with Durkheim's emphasis on anomie, without breakdown and collapse there will be no progress.

Alternatively, chaos theory emphasises the chaotic in the universe, that science is not as predictable as often thought. As translated to criminology, the status quo is in fact chaotic and crime and disorder are normal in society. Order is the unusual or deviant situation. For instance, according to postmodern criminologists Stuart Henry and Dragan Milovanovic:

> [rather than] privileging order, chaos theorists privilege disorder; order is but the deviant case. In chaos theory's description of social structure, far-from-equilibrium conditions and non-linear dynamics exist where chance, spontaneity, and a degree of indeterminacy prevail. In chaos theory, non-linearity means that disproportional outcomes can arise such that small inputs can produce large effects. (Henry and Milovanovic, 1996: 46)

The classic illustration of chaos theory at work is the butterfly effect, where the flapping of a butterfly's wings (a small input) may in principle lead to a tornado on the other side of the planet (a large effect) (see Lorenz, 2000). According to Milovanovic (1997: vii) 'The world is more disorderly, uncertain, non-linear, and unpredictable' than is claimed by the natural sciences and by modernism; but again, this is not necessarily a bad thing. For Milovanovic, this chaos: '… is not without form and structure: rather, the notion of an orderly disorder [is] the basis of an alternative metaphysics. Chaos should not, therefore, be seen as purely randomness and chance events' (1997: vii).

Put simply, what is generally perceived as disordered or chaotic may in itself represent an alternative form of order, what Milovanovic called an 'orderly disorder'. Translated to the criminological context, different representations and expectations of order can lead to competing claims concerning order and disorder and the use and function of public space. Yet, despite the possibility of an 'orderly disorder', for society to operate there needs to be some shared recognition of the importance of social order, albeit with a degree of tolerance of different perspectives and an appreciation that understandings of order may change. The importance of social order is considered next.

The importance of social order

One way to consider the usefulness of social order is to contemplate how life would be without it. An example is the order required to drive on the road. If there were no laws of the road and everyone was free to do whatever they wanted, then people would be found driving outside of any lanes, maybe towards each other on the same side of the road at great speed. Initially there might be chaos, yet many drivers would soon discover that to survive they would have to slow down considerably as everyone else on the road would be expected to do the unexpected. A new 'orderly disorder' could result, but it would not be as efficient – or safe – as the one where we are told which side of the road to drive on and at what speeds. And there is still the possibility that some drivers would not adhere to this new norm of the road. For this reason ordering for coordination is still usually preferable. According to Hechter and Horne (2009: 1):

> Coordination requires that people develop stable expectations about others' behavior. When driving, for example, it is helpful to know whether others are likely to approach you on the right or the left side of the road. If you and I agree to a date Friday at 8:00 p.m., we presume that we are referring to the same time zone and calendar and that we will each be at the same place at the specified time.

For ordered living there need to be stable expectations; although, as Hechter and Horne (2009: 1) point out, 'We can have stable expectations and still not much social order'. The example they use is Afghanistan where the stable expectations are 'frequent interethnic violence, highly unequal relations between the genders and age grades, and a meager standard of living' (2009: 1). It is arguable that this is a form of social order (or orderly disorder), but not necessarily the kind of social order most of us would request. Thus, for social order to be *acceptable* there need to be stable expectations and normative values that are generally morally tolerable.

The question is whose ideas of social order and morally right behaviour take precedence? Order can be hierarchical requiring deference from those regarded as lower down the social order (see also Chapter Seven). British society, for example, has a heritage that is highly structured and hierarchical, although automatic deference to one's superiors has diminished over the past century. In the years after the First World War class barriers were already weakening. According to Robert Roberts (1971/1990: 221) 'Labourers and even the "no class" who only a few years before had "known their place" and kept to it … seemed no longer willing to return to the ranks of servility' (see also Cannadine, 1998). By the time of the 1920s Great Depression and resultant mass unemployment there was further '[b]luring of the social layers', but this was a 'parity in wretchedness' which bred a shared understanding (Roberts, 1971/1990: 223). Post Second World War there was further diminishment of subordination with fewer people willing to accept a lower status.

Yet fast-forward to the 21st century and there are still some who expect and demand respect simply because of their social standing. Contemporary elites are not always the most obvious. In addition to directors of multinational conglomerates the powerful might include TV celebrities, super-rich footballers, politicians, or even cultural commentators who claim to have superior tastes to the rest of us. As noted in Chapter Four, Pierre Bourdieu (1979/1984) traced a cultural aristocracy of taste with the tastes of the 'ruling' classes regarded as legitimate, whereas lower tastes are seen as middle brow or merely the 'popular' tastes of the masses. There may even be sub-popular tastes below this (Millie, 2008; 2016). Those with the required cultural capital, educational level and occupation dictate which tastes are legitimate and which are not.

Such a perspective matches that of Karl Marx who – to simplify his position – saw society as ordered between those who own the means of production and those who just own their labour. In this context society is understood as a neat divide between the powerful and the powerless with a new social order only possible through revolution. In late modern society the picture is not so simple; but the basic premise that a few demand respect from the rest of us is maintained. Whether they get that respect is another thing. Respect is explored in more detail in Chapter Seven.

Just as some 'elites' demand respect, it is possible that some people like the idea of a strict hierarchy and knowing how they fit into this (even if this is lower down the social order). Certain strands of analytic philosophy, for example, seek predictability and find beauty in everything being in its correct place and order. The conservative philosopher Roger Scruton (2009: 80) has talked about the pleasure of neat rows of vegetables that 'satisfy our need for visual order'. Bertrand Russell too found beauty in mathematic predictability: '[Mathematics] gives in absolute perfection that combination, characteristic of great art, of godlike freedom, with a sense of inevitable density; because, in fact, it constructs an ideal world where everything is perfect and yet true' (Russell, 1967: 158–9).

Yet those with lower tastes are condescended to by those above them (Korsmeyer, 2005). The activities of those deemed to be of a lower social order may even be criminalised. In such instances social ordering is not to the benefit of all. Yet, as noted, for us to live together rather than in separate individual 'bubbles' there needs to be some understanding of social order. Various philosophers have attempted to answer the question of how we can live together and it is to this that I now turn.

Living together

According to classic free market philosophy social and economic cooperation is made more possible through a division of labour leading to the generation of maximum wealth for the nation (see for instance Adam Smith, 1776 and Émile Durkheim, 1893/2014). While recognising the intrinsic need for all levels of employment, the downside of such a division of labour is that it requires some people to have lower employment and, therefore, lower social status. We live together more effectively, but at the expense of equality of status.

As was noted in Chapter Three, Thomas Hobbes (1651/1990) was pessimistic about our ability to cooperate and live together unless it is in our self-interest to do so. Social contract philosophers, such as Hobbes, Bentham, Locke and Rousseau saw the political contract between the state and the citizen as the key way to engender an ordered society. It is a consequentialist philosophy that sees our self-interest served by working together and with the state. In short, in order for people with different perspectives and beliefs to live together there needs to be an unspoken agreement of obligation to cooperate among citizens and the state, while sacrificing some freedoms to gain state protection. The social contract is considered in more detail in the following chapter on rules. What is important to note here is that, through a social contract, social order is thought possible with state intervention.

Free market philosophy sometimes assumes that order is possible without any state involvement, especially within markets. I return here to the earlier example of a road without any markings or speed restrictions. It was suggested that initially there would be chaos, but that a new 'orderly disorder' may eventually prevail with drivers accepting the need to slow down, realising that everyone else will do something unexpected. This unexpectedness itself then becomes a form of order (or orderly disorder). Drawing on the work of neoliberal economist Friedrich Hayek (2013) this could also be seen as a form of 'spontaneous order' that can emerge as the result of individuals' uncoordinated actions; or to quote the Scottish philosopher Adam Ferguson (1767/1992: 119), 'the result of human action, but not the execution of any human design'. Adam Smith (1776) talked in terms of an 'invisible hand' suggesting that the apparent chaos of economic markets is self-regulating and becomes ordered by individuals pursuing self-interest. Thus, in the example of unrestricted driving, each driver has the self-interest of getting to their destination in one piece and so drives cautiously and slows down. The limitation of the idea of 'spontaneous order' is that it assumes a degree of rational thinking and that each individual driver will come to the same conclusion. As noted, some drivers may still drive assuming that everyone else will get out of their way – driving in their own 'bubble' – potentially resulting in disaster. Spontaneous order also has its limitations when applied to markets and the assumption that they will self-correct (see also Stedman Jones, 2014). If nothing else, the financial crisis of 2007–8 proved that non-intervention in capitalist systems can be a big mistake. Without intervention in the markets some sort of spontaneous order *may* have been found, but this 'natural' order might not have been beneficial for society at large. For any meaningful and sustainable order within markets (or on roads, or in any other social situation) self-interest only gets you so far; there needs to be concern for the interests of others. If concern for others cannot be guaranteed then there needs to be some sort of intervention or regulation, and this may be by the state. Just as intervention is sometimes needed in disorderly capitalist markets, then so too is intervention needed in order to maintain social order in our daily lives. This is the role of the state and of state actors such as the police.

Maintaining order

The police are recognised as having three related functions. The first of these is law enforcement and relates to the kind of activities most associated with the police as crime fighters. While she was UK Home Secretary, Theresa May (2011) was of the opinion that this is the most important function for the police, stating that 'We need them to be the tough, no-nonsense crime-fighters they signed up to become'. May had a particularly narrow conception of police function (Millie, 2013); however, there is much more that the police do. The second is a social service function, recognising that much of what the police do is not related directly to 'fighting crime', but entails reassuring the community, dealing with mental health issues or perhaps working with schools. The visible and politically attractive 'bobby on the beat' is part of the police's social service function in that the patrolling officer is unlikely to deal with much actual crime (Clarke and Hough, 1984; Millie, 2013), but will fulfil a social service in reassuring the public that the police are there, and may intervene if required. The third function of the police, and the one of most relevance to this chapter, is the maintenance of public order. This can be demonstrated on the grand scale through tackling riotous crowds or at a more mundane level 'the settlement of conflicts, potentially crimes, by means other than formal law enforcement' (Reiner, 2013: 166).

In terms of the type of order the police are asked to maintain, according to Canadian criminologist Richard Ericson (1982), they are there to reproduce the order of the status quo. In the UK this is reflected in the instruction to maintain the Queen's peace. Mike Brogden and Graham Ellison (2013: 9) have claimed that 'state policing has always been committed to maintaining a divisive social order'. Whether this is true or not, the police's maintenance of order is a conservative function, to maintain a social order that is acceptable to those with requisite political capital; and these are the powerful rather than the powerless.

This may be problematic during times of anomie or social change. On a more day-to-day level, anyone or anything that challenges the status quo – the generally accepted idea of an ordered society as dictated by those with power – may face censure. One area where this can occur is with expectations of aesthetic order where people or things that do not adhere to an expected aesthetic for a particular spatial and temporal context may be removed and/or criminalised. Building on discussions of aesthetics covered in Chapter Four, the idea of an aesthetic order is considered next.

Aesthetic order

According to the sociologist Richard Sennett people's aspirations can be regarded as 'a search for purity' (1970: 9). In other words, humans often wish to perceive the social world and themselves by pushing away the dirt (see also Sibley, 1995). What is left is an aesthetically ordered life where those regarded as impure or dirty are out of sight. This view is similar to Scruton's (2009) observation about pleasure being found in neat rows of vegetables with the removal of weeds and vegetables that are out of line, or Russell's (1967) aesthetic appreciation of mathematic predictability. What is sought is an aesthetic order. Ruth Lorand (2000) used the term 'aesthetic order' in her work on the philosophy of order in beauty and art. Here the phrase is used to reflect an expressed need for aesthetic order in the world around us, be that an orderly urban environment or perhaps a rurality where everything is in its correct place (Millie, 2016). For instance, and as noted in Chapter Four, the apparent wilderness of National Parks is often highly regulated and ordered where the more 'wild' qualities may be manufactured in order to create the image that is expected (Hermer, 2002). Within the city various planning departments and others with power (such as major employers, politicians, retail chains and city centre managers) demand a city that is predictable and ordered in a way that pleases the consuming majority (Bannister et al, 2006) and thereby maximises profit. People or things that interfere with the aesthetic that is expected by the consuming majority are taken out of the equation.

Having said this, the everyday lived realities for many people can be more disordered and chaotic (see de Certeau, 1984). Urban spaces in particular can be sites for spontaneity, amazement and carnival (Presdee, 2000). Yet, the apparent aesthetic disorder of the everyday could be regarded as an alternative order (or an orderly disorder), but just labelled as disorderly by those with power. Writing about Greenwich Village in New York the urbanist Jane Jacobs (1961/1992) had a particularly romantic view of 'traditional' urban living, which maybe seemed chaotic to the outsider, but worked as an orderly whole for those who lived and worked there:

> … wherever the old city is working successfully, is a marvellous order for maintaining the safety of the streets and the freedom of the city … . This order is all composed of movement and change, and … we may fancifully call it the art form of the city and liken it to a dance – not to a simple-minded precision dance with everyone kicking up at the same time, twirling in unison and bowing off en masse, but to an intricate ballet in which the individual dancers and ensembles all have distinctive parts which miraculously reinforce each other and compose an orderly whole. (1961/1992: 50)

Such orderly disorder cannot be assumed of neighbourhoods and it is not easy to reproduce. There is a normative expectation that each individual will recognise the value of the others in the dance and will allow space for others' expression. Jacobs's view of city life is appealing, but late modern urbanity is often composed of different dancers performing different dances which may or may not complement one another (Millie, 2016). Where we cannot rely on neighbourliness, those with power have created various normative, municipal and criminal rules with the aim of creating everyday aesthetic order – ranging from litter by-laws through to zoning ordinances (see Valverde, 2012). For Alison Young (2014: 43) the resultant legislated city is born of 'a desire to control the city's perceived unruliness and fecklessness'.

The power to define an acceptable aesthetic order is evident in the much critiqued 'broken windows' perspective of James Q Wilson and George Kelling (1982) which led to various forms of order maintenance policing (for example Harcourt, 2001; Mitchell, 2003; Ferrell, 2006). According to Jeff Ferrell (2006: 261–2), 'broken windows' is 'essentially an aesthetic analysis of crime's etiology'. For Wilson and Kelling, broken windows – or low-level disorders more broadly – if left unrepaired communicate neighbourhood decline, causing 'good' citizens to withdraw from the streets, resulting in less informal control and crime taking root. The low-level disorders in question would include people deemed to interfere with the aesthetic order of the street, such as street homeless people or perhaps young people congregating in groups. Such censure of 'disordered' people has been criticised. For instance, according to Don Mitchell: '[T]his defence of punitive measures against homeless people simply asserts that the *aesthetics of place* outweigh other considerations, such as the right of homeless people to find a means to live, to sleep, *to be*' (Mitchell, 2001: 68, emphasis in original).

'Broken windows' has proved attractive because it is simple and has led to various experiments in 'order maintenance' policing. Yet, a causal relationship between 'disorder' and crime has been questioned (Sampson and Raudenbush, 1999; Harcourt, 2001). Furthermore, according to Bernard Harcourt, 'the meaning of order and disorder may not be as stable or as fixed as the order maintenance approach suggests' (2001: 18). For example, graffiti and street art are not always read as disorders (Ferrell, 1996; 2006; Millie, 2008; 2014b; Snyder, 2009; Young, 2014). In fact, in some districts graffiti and street art are attractors for tourists and entrepreneurs and can be *positive* elements in processes of gentrification. In Toronto, for example, street art occurring along Queen Street West or Kensington Market may go unpunished as it adds to the 'alternative' aesthetic favoured by many retailers locating there (Millie, 2011). If the street art or graffiti were in more sensitive commercial or business districts, they would more likely be seen as a nuisance and removed. In London under the Queen Elizabeth Hall at the Southbank Centre, graffiti was initially tolerated but is now actively encouraged, becoming a tourist draw to the area (Millie, 2009a). In Melbourne Australia, graffiti and street art are tolerated in the laneways of the city (Young, 2010). In fact, according to Alison Young (2012: 299) 'Tourism Victoria has included shots of Melbourne's street art in its promotional materials, and street art often appears in areas experiencing gentrification rather than social decline'. Yet, at the other extreme, many graffiti writers have ended up in prison. Notions of aesthetic order will vary, it seems, depending on place and time contexts, and by appropriateness to attract tourists.

Thus, despite the assertions of Wilson and Kelling, 'aesthetic' order and disorder are not ontologically fixed and are instead social constructions that vary depending on spatial and temporal contexts. For Charis Kubrin (2008: 206), '[t]he social construction of disorder and the dichotomizing of the orderly versus disorderly can have serious consequences'. In the right context graffiti and street art may be 'orderly disorders'. Out of place, they may be seen as disorders to be censured. A simple list of unacceptable disorders becomes less meaningful when apparent disorder is loathed by some but celebrated by others, or accepted on one street but unacceptable in a different context (Millie, 2008). As before, it is a question of who decides and this is often tied with issues of taste and power.

Conclusions

Criminology is intrinsically concerned with questions of order and disorder. What this chapter has demonstrated is that closer engagement with philosophy can shed light on people's conceptions of order, and the mechanisms in place to make order more likely. The chapter started with a quote from Bart Simpson, that it is "My bubble, my rules". As noted, his view got to the heart of the ethical egoism of late modernity. Neoliberal capitalism has promoted the individual to the extent that we are frequently ignorant of our impact on others – or worse, we do not really care about the effect of our actions on others. Yet we do not live in isolation. The challenge is how social existence can be encouraged in a society of individuals. The Biblical instruction to 'Love your neighbour as yourself' was noted as a good place to start, although of course many would find religious instruction off-putting. We construct various ordering devices to make sense of the world around us. For instance, the classification of actions or omissions as crimes creates an order between law abiders and law breakers. Yet, as this chapter has highlighted, the reality is that we are all law breakers or breakers of various normative rules to varying degrees.

Criminological understanding of social order draws a lot from the philosophy of Émile Durkheim whose work highlighted the disorder and crime associated with periods of anomie, or normlessness. During such periods of change – whether these are periods of economic growth or downturn – new ways of living become evident which challenge existing norms and values. Society struggles to come to terms with this change while trying to keep hold of the past. During periods of anomie what is defined as criminal may change as society changes. For Durkheim crime is a normal part of society. In fact, it is a necessary part of social progress as we challenge the status quo. Nonetheless, when new ways of living have a harmful impact on others, then classification of such changes as disorder or crime may still be the right thing to do – although defining 'harm' is not always simple.

Certain philosophers see order straightforwardly as a good thing, to the extent that Roger Scruton (2009: 80) has talked about the appealing neatness of rows of vegetables, and Bertrand Russell (1967) found beauty in the predictability of mathematics. Yet, Durkheim did not see order as set in stone. This is similarly the view from postmodern philosophy. For instance, according to catastrophe theory, breakdown and collapse are fundamental to the evolution of systems – including social systems. Chaos theory suggests that *dis*order is in fact the status quo. Just as Durkheim had discovered, crime and disorder are normal in society. Milovanovic (1997) identified an 'orderly disorder', that what is perceived as disordered may in fact represent an alternative order. This is an important point for criminology. What is labelled as disordered behaviour may represent order to those given the label. It is a question of who gets to define what is regarded as ordered and what is disordered.

The influence of power is a theme that is common to much of this book, and social status certainly has an influence in defining an ordered society. For instance, although universal deference has declined, there are still those that perceive of themselves as being of a higher social order, more than willing to dictate what they regard as the requirements for an ordered society. That said, some form of order is still a good thing. Earlier in this chapter the example of an ordered road was given, where there are certain legal and normative requirements to driving which make the experience more pleasurable (and less likely to result in serious injury). This is order for coordination. This does not negate the possibility of alternative conceptions of order; however, in many circumstances there need to be generally accepted standards.

Also considered were ways we can live, work and trade together in a situation of social order. The role of a social contract was highlighted. According to free market economic philosophy (for example Hayek, 2013) order is maintained in markets as they are self-regulating through 'spontaneous order'. The recent economic crisis has demonstrated the limits to this way of thinking and the benefits of informed intervention. Of relevance to criminology, once we realise that order does not 'spontaneously' emerge, then there is a role for criminal justice and financial regulation agencies in policing markets. The self-interest that fuels financial markets – and which meant that Bart Simpson could live within his bubble – would only get us so far. Such individualism would never lead to a social order of equals and, perhaps, this is where the state needs to intervene. How order can be maintained is another issue. The police have an order maintenance function, but as Ericson (1982) has highlighted, this is a conservative function leading to the maintenance of the status quo. If the state has a role, then there needs also to be room to question existing conceptions of order, to consider 'what ought to be' as much as 'what is' (see also Bennett, 2015: 131).

One area where conceptions of order are constantly being questioned is in terms of aesthetic order. The preferred look and feel of cities is often maintained through aesthetic regulation, with certain tastes promoted and others censured. Similarly, the aesthetic order of more rural or apparently wilderness locations is often only possible through regulation and criminalisation of un-aesthetic development. As noted, this is not necessarily a bad thing; however, it is again a question of who decides what is acceptable, tolerable or censurable.

Notes

[1]   I have used this quote a number of times in my work (for example 2009a; 2009b) and I make no apology for using it again here. Truss has summed up one of the key concerns for criminology and for moral philosophy, simply how do we live together?

SIX

Rules

Introduction

In political and policy rhetoric there is much talk of 'playing by the rules'. For instance, in the US Barak Obama declared in his 2010 State of the Union address that, 'we should ... enforce our laws, and ensure that everyone who plays by the rules can contribute to our economy and enrich our nation'. Similarly, in the UK during his successful 2010 election campaign David Cameron claimed, 'We're fighting the fact that people who do the right thing, who work hard, who save, who play by the rules get hit by the system'. Six years earlier Tony Blair (2004) suggested that: '[People] want a community where the decent law-abiding majority are in charge; where those that play by the rules do well; and those that don't, get punished'. According to this narrative 'playing by the rules' is a duty, a responsibility; and 'doing the right thing' is a prerequisite for contemporary citizenship that should be rewarded. There is a simple dichotomy between a law-abiding 'us' and a rule breaking 'them'; and if Obama is right, playing by the rules may also be associated with a person's economic contribution.

The political use of this sort of narrative is very powerful. Politicians present a persuasive story where they are on the side of those who work hard, keep the law and obey society's various rules and standards – the mythical moral, or law-abiding, majority – while also being intolerant of those who do not adhere to these rules. The imagined connection between elected and electorate is maintained. But what does it mean to play by the rules in contemporary Western capitalist society? The idea of obeying the law – which is clearly a more formalised interpretation of playing by the rules – tends to be conflated with compliance with other 'sub-legal' norms and values which are perhaps morally, socially or economically (but not necessarily legally) required. However, as highlighted in the previous chapter, people who would regard themselves as law-abiding can also be guilty of breaking rules, be they breaches of law or other normative standards. Such breaches may include, for instance, motorway speeding, tax avoidance, minor fraud or unauthorised parking (Chenery et al, 1999; Karstedt and Farrall, 2006; Millie, 2008; Wells, 2012). The UK parliamentary expenses scandal of 2009, the global banking crisis of 2008 onwards and the Volkswagen emissions scandal of 2015 all demonstrate that politicians and corporations can also stretch the limits of 'playing by the rules'. The banking crisis in particular was driven by a system that encouraged risk to the extent that financial law and moral boundaries were pushed to extremes. In sports also, in 2015 the governing bodies of world football and world athletics were both hit by allegations of corruption and cheating. It seems playing by the rules is not straightforward, especially when there are opportunities to bend or break the rules for personal gain. Exceptions to rules can also sometime be found.

In this chapter the philosophy of rules and rule adherence is considered, and its relevance to criminology. The chapter starts with social contract theory. The chapter then considers rules as moral goods and rights, including the possibility of natural law. Rule adherence is questioned, as is the need to obey every normative and legal rule. It is contended that the morally right thing to do might sometimes be to break certain rules. The chapter also looks at situations when it is acceptable to bend rules, or when there are exceptions to rules. In such situations game theory might be a useful way to understand how rules are played out in late modernity.

Social contracts

In Chapter Three the relevance of moral philosophy to criminology was considered. Here the focus is the relevance of a social contract for cooperative and moral living, and therefore by extension to criminology. According to Christopher Bennett (2015: 131), some might argue that '[i]f there were no society ... there would be no morality'. However, this view is limited:

> The problem with this sociological view of morality is that it concludes that morality is nothing more than whichever rules happen to be adopted by a particular society. It allows for no standard by which we could evaluate the different moralities that societies adopt. It would simply be a theory of 'what is' rather than ... 'what ought to be'. (2015: 131)

What is needed is a way to acknowledge that how we live morally is socially constructed, but also that there may be ideal standards. The focus here is the social construction of morality as expressed though social contract theory. A social contract is enacted between citizens and state emphasising moral action judged by adherence to an agreed set of rules. By focusing on rule adherence social contract theory is deontological. It is also consequentialist in that it stresses the consequences of sticking to or breaking these rules.

According to Jean-Jacques Rousseau (1762/2003) the rules and laws created reflect the general 'will of the people', an idea similar to Émile Durkheim's (1893/2014) 'collective conscience'. As noted previously, Thomas Hobbes (1651/1990) was of the view that self-interest was at the heart of any attempt to engender cooperative action. The limit of this perspective is that it ignores non-self-interested or altruistic action. David Hume did not see this necessarily as a problem. His view was that, while altruism is possible, natural sympathies are limited; as Bennett (2015) has noted:

> The parent may sacrifice himself for his child, but he won't tend to be willing to assume the same burden for the sake of someone else's child. The soldier may be prepared to risk death for the security or glory of his own nation, but tends to be less willing to do so for the sake of humanity in general.

In Chapter Two Paul Ricoeur was cited regarding a Christian 'economy of gift and its logic of superabundance' (1990: 395). Building on the Golden Rule the economy of gift is that you choose to treat others with love and mercy, even if you do not expect it in return. It is a perspective that is not dependent on any familial or social bond or loyalty. This may be an ideal and Hobbes' view is the other extreme, 'a kind of lowest-common-denominator view of morality' (Bennett, 2015: 138). In our everyday moral dealings with others we find that people act out of selfish interest or through natural sympathies to particular individuals or groups. From a criminological perspective there is clear potential for selfish or preferential action to lead to harmful or criminal impacts on others. Yet people also behave altruistically, aiding others without expectation of anything in return. The place of a social contract is to recognise non-selfish cooperation, while putting in place a set of rules that uses people's inclinations for selfish action to make social cooperation more likely than social harm or criminality.

The social contract is the basis for democratic government. Put simply, a democratic election ought to ensure that the party that most represents the will of the people is given power to create rules that reflect the will of the people. At a fundamental level this arrangement has clear benefits for community living. Yet, there are potential problems, not least the possibility that those elected may ignore the general will, or might intervene too much in individual lives. There is also a danger that the general will may itself be inward looking, or biased against certain groups or outsiders, thus electing politicians that reflect their particular prejudicial values.

At a time of plural beliefs and global movements there are pressures to create international rules and laws based on the common interests and the general will of the planet. The various United Nations conventions and agreements reflect this desire, but, as will be discussed, there are ways of breaking or bending such rules. Clearly, any form of social contract is not an easy task. It also assumes that most people know the rules in the first place. According to Rousseau, there is an additional free-rider problem:

> In fact, each individual, as a man, may have a particular will contrary or dissimilar to the general will which he has as a citizen. His particular interest may speak to him quite differently from the common interest: his absolute and naturally independent existence may make him look upon what he owes to the common cause as a gratuitous contribution, the loss of which will do no less harm to others than the payment of it is burdensome to himself … he may wish to enjoy the rights of citizenship without being ready to fulfil the duties of a subject. (Rousseau, 1762/2003: 11)

Contemporary politicians often use this language of rights and responsibilities. For instance, in the UK the former Labour Prime Minister Tony Blair once proposed a political agenda centred on the concept of 'respect' (on which more in the next chapter), and that this respect was focused on a reciprocal arrangement between individual rights and collective responsibilities. According to Blair: 'Respect is at the heart of a belief in society. It is what makes us a community, not merely a group of isolated individuals. It makes real a new contract between citizen and state, a contract that says that with rights and opportunities come responsibilities and obligations' (2002).

Blair used the language of a social contract based on respect between all parties. Whether the state always shows respect to all citizens is another matter (Millie, 2009b). More recently, the former Conservative Prime Minister David Cameron has similarly talked of rights and responsibilities, but this time emphasising a narrative of moral decline:

Do we have the determination to confront the slow-motion moral collapse that has taken place in parts of our country these past few generations? Irresponsibility. Selfishness. Behaving as if your choices have no consequences. Children without fathers. Schools without discipline. Reward without effort. Crime without punishment. Rights without responsibilities. Communities without control. (Cameron, 2011)

Their emphasis was slightly different, but both Labour and the Conservatives had assumed that Britain was experiencing moral decline. It is debatable whether morals have actually been declining (see for instance, Pearson, 1983; Millie, 2009b); however, what is significant is that the supposed solution was state-enforced moral improvement (Millie, 2010). The Conservatives claimed to want less state control with a bottom-up approach to solving problems, labelled as 'the Big Society'. For instance, the Conservative Party manifesto for the 2010 election contained the slogan 'Big Society Not Big Government' (the Conservative Party, 2010: 36). The reality was that less state control translated into major budget cuts for government departments, while still enacting legislation from above in order to enforce behavioural improvement (for instance the Anti-social Behaviour, Crime and Policing Act 2014). One half of the social contract was maintained (that of creating rules), but the connection between state and citizen was left in a fragile state.

In late modern society there is a tendency for social control to take precedence over any meaningful social contract between state and citizen. Rule adherence is enforced rather than negotiated. And, as has been highlighted in previous chapters, the 'normal' position is that individuals or groups with sufficient political capital or power have greatest say in dictating the values and rules that take precedence; as was once sung by Canadian singer-songwriter Bruce Cockburn:

Person in the street shrugs – 'Security comes first'
But the trouble with normal is it always gets worse. (1983)[1]

The powerless are left with diminished influence with more restrictions put on their lives and increased criminalisation.

The response to the status quo, for many, has been non-compliance and this has formed the backbone for much criminological work, from the early sociology of deviance (for example Becker, 1963; Erikson, 1966), through to subcultural theory (for example Hebdige,

1979) and more recent work within cultural criminology (Ferrell and Sanders, 1995). The question is whether non-compliance or even civil disobedience and breach of the social contract are always wrong, or whether there are occasions when they are the morally right thing to do.

For Socrates, by living within a particular society we have a duty to obey its laws, even if these are unjust; as Paul Smith has highlighted, 'Socrates argued, if one does not accept the laws, one can emigrate' (2008: 36). The basis of this thinking is that by living within a particular jurisdiction we are tacitly consenting to its laws. The problem of such a perspective is that it assumes one can emigrate, and it negates the possibility that unjust laws ought to be challenged from within. Emigration may solve the problem for you, but not for those left behind. That said, there are ways to challenge the laws of a country without putting others in danger. In October 2015 a 15-year-old boy shot and killed a police employee in Parramatta, Western Sydney, Australia, in what was labelled a politically motivated terrorist attack. The victim was leaving the New South Wales Police Headquarters. In a speech following the attack Australian Prime Minister Malcolm Turnbull echoed Socrates in stating: 'It is not compulsory to live in Australia, if you find Australian values are, you know, unpalatable, then there's a big wide world out there and people have got freedom of movement' (ABC News, 2015a).

A similar sentiment was expressed by the Chair of the Parramatta Mosque, that 'If you don't like Australia, leave' (ABC News, 2015b) Yet elsewhere in his speech Turnbull referred to the Golden Rule and 'this fundamental value of mutual respect' that is important to Australian life; 'you might call it live-and-let-live, we respect each other' (ABC News, 2015a). The idea of respect is explored in the next chapter. The important point here is that the social contract is something that ought to be challenged, even if this is through non-compliance and, on occasion, civil disobedience. But this challenge needs to be in a way that demonstrates respect for others. Respect is something that concerned Immanuel Kant (1785/1990) who developed Socrates' ideas by suggesting that to act morally people must act through duty. However, duty is not the same as blindly following the state's rules and laws. One's duty may be to question the status quo.

Rules as moral goods and rights

'Playing by the rules' is a deontological concern. It is a narrative that dictates the goodness or badness of actions and omissions, with adherence to 'the rules' a clear duty or prerequisite of citizenship. The rules are both legal and normative and structure our everyday existence. As considered in Chapter Two, GE Moore's intuitionism was that 'Good is good, and that is the end of the matter' (1903/2005: 7). Yet normative and legal rules are human made and therefore imperfect. In other words, the law cannot, by definition, be absolutely good. Saying something is good and correspondingly that something else is bad is rarely the end of the matter.

That said, many laws are based on universal ideas as reflected in the Golden Rule – what for some would be regarded as natural laws (for example the work of Cicero or Thomas Aquinas) (see also Kelsen, 1934/1967; Finnis, 2011). For instance, it is universally – or at least generally – agreed that it is wrong to kill another human. Yet when this idea is written down in law and then acted out in the real world this apparently simple rule is made more complicated, with a distinction made between murder and manslaughter. In some jurisdictions there is also something called justifiable homicide where killing another human is seen as defensible, for instance in the case of self-defence. Furthermore, there are different rules for the killing of humans by military personnel during times of war, whether the dead are seen as 'combatants' or civilians. If one is to play by the rules then it is important to realise that there are exceptions to these rules (Edgerton, 1985).

This complicated picture does not disprove the idea of natural law. Killing another is ordinarily a morally bad thing to do, but how it is interpreted by imperfect people is not going to be straightforward. In his classic work of Christian apologetics, *Mere Christianity*, CS Lewis (1952) argued that, despite differences between civilisations and the times in which we live, all humans have in common a law of human nature that underpins how we think we ought to live our lives. All humans have also in common the fact that they break this law of nature:

> First, that human beings, all over the earth, have this curious idea that they ought to behave in a certain way, and cannot really get rid of it. Secondly, that they do not in fact behave in that way. They know the Law of Nature; they break it. These two facts are the foundation of all clear thinking about ourselves and the universe we live in. (1952: 8)

According to Lewis the law of nature comes from God. Others may say it is reflective of society's mores that are passed down from generation to generation (Sumner, 1906/1940). For Hans Kelsen (1934/1967) such a law may be a 'Grundnorm' or basic norm upon which all our laws are built.

Arguing that there are basic or natural laws is not the same as Moore's intuitionism, that 'good is good'. It is saying that *some* basic goods are always good, but beyond this is the law as written where there is room for interpretation. According to Cicero (54–51BC/1928: 210) 'True [or natural] law is right reason in agreement with nature; it is of universal application, unchanging and everlasting'. Outside of this is law that is human made, imperfect and can be changed. An example used by Joel Feinberg (1979) is the law that existed in 19th-century America prohibiting the assistance of fugitive slaves, or the law in Nazi Germany on not aiding Jews. The notion of legal rule adherence as a duty is put in doubt, with the morally right – or naturally good – thing being non-compliance and to assist those in need. Perhaps in such instances the only duty is to natural law rather than the law as written? In short, just because something is illegal does not make it wrong; and similarly, if something is legal does not make it right.

The existence or absence of natural law is a metaphysical or religious concern in that it deals with the abstract nature or rules of existence. For some, such as the utilitarian Jeremy Bentham, we should not concern ourselves with metaphysical or religious speculation regarding natural law or natural rights. Instead we need to focus on practical ways to maximise overall happiness. In fact, Bentham famously stated that 'natural rights is simple nonsense: natural and imprescriptible rights, rhetorical nonsense, nonsense upon stilts' (in Schofield et al, 2002: 330). More recent legal positivism has been equally scathing about natural law and rights. For instance, according to HLA Hart (1961/2012) law is a social construction and everything that is within the law is there 'because some person or group put it there, either intentionally or accidentally' (Green, 2012: xviii). Law has a history, it can be changed and it is known (or knowable). Law certainly has a history and it changes as society's moral and normative values change – notable examples from the 20th century include prohibition laws on alcohol and laws related to homosexuality. Alternatively, unchanging natural laws are seen as 'the sort of spooky stuff that Bentham derided' (Moore, 1992: 188). In reference to Cicero's view of natural law, Linda Green has claimed 'It is hard to find legal theorists who still believe all of this' (2012: xviii).

Nonetheless, there are legal scholars who take on board at least part of natural law theory, most notably Ronald Dworkin (1977). Legal positivists such as Hart (1961/2012) and Joseph Raz (2009) have taken a view that law's validity is not dependent on its morality. Dworkin was critical of this position and instead saw law as grounded in morality, even if this interpretation of morality is sometimes misguided. His view is that some people's moral principles can be wrong. Similarly, the laws enacted by people can also be wrong and the morally right thing to do in such circumstances is to disobey the law; as Smith has put it, 'When a law wrongly invades someone's moral rights, they have the right to break that law' (2008: 38). Dworkin saw rights as trumping non-rights objectives, even if these are written in law. Examples would include the assistance of fugitive slaves, or aiding of Jews in Nazi Germany already mentioned. John Stuart Mill highlighted the importance of rights in 1859; that 'If all mankind minus one were of one opinion, mankind would be no more justified in silencing that one person than he, if he had the power, would be in silencing mankind' (Mill 1859/2002: 20).

The notion of rights is a particular interpretation of natural law that gained prominence following the American Revolution and the signing of the US Constitution (1787), and in the 20th century following the Second World War, culminating in the 1948 Universal Declaration. The aim of the Universal Declaration was 'recognition of the inherent dignity and of the equal and inalienable rights of all members of the human family [which] is the foundation of freedom, justice and peace in the world' (United Nations, 1948). Although the Declaration is clearly a social construction, the idea that each of us has inherent dignity and rights has a lot in common with the notion of natural law. To give one example in relation to the earlier discussion of killing, Article 3 of the Declaration states 'Everyone has the right to life, liberty and security of person.' Of course, how the Declaration is played out in different jurisdictions is another issue and may make the idea of rights a mere aspiration for many.

Bending rules and exceptions to rules

As already noted, killing someone is clearly a moral wrong (and a crime); yet killing during wartime is regarded by some as a necessary evil. Going up to someone and assaulting them is quite rightly criminalised; yet within the boxing ring it is a required part of the sport (see Groombridge, 2016). Even if many find boxing morally repugnant, it is legal – within the rules of boxing's various governing bodies – and an accepted part of late modern life. Thus, for what appear to be absolute moral wrongs, there are exceptions (Edgerton, 1985) or occasions when rules can be bent (Hinde, 2007). According to Robert A Hinde (2007) our everyday experiences allow for a degree of flexibility in how morality is acted out. For instance:

> ... in the commercial world people do the best they can
> for themselves, in war soldiers kill, politicians distort
> the truth to please the electorate, and barristers defend
> individuals whom they believe to be guilty or prosecute
> ones they believe to be innocent. Seen from the standpoint
> of everyday morality, they are breaking the Golden Rule,
> yet not only does the businessman, soldier, politician, or
> barrister believe him- or herself to be doing the right thing
> but, to different degrees, their behaviour is accepted by
> others. (Hinde, 2007: 1)

Thus, while there may be natural laws and generally agreed moral
principles, there is often an element of grey in how everyday use
of rules and laws is played out. The law itself operates through a
system of exceptions. Examples include taking account of poor
health, intoxication or emotional stress, or perhaps of a person's age,
gender or disability (Edgerton, 1985: 5). A clear example is the age
of criminal responsibility. Only above this age have you committed
a 'crime', although the actions of those below this age may be the
same. Furthermore, in England and Wales – as elsewhere – various
rationales are used by the police in the recording of crime. Often a
subjective decision is made in determining whether an act or omission
is classed as a crime or 'no crime'. If a case gets as far as prosecution, the
decision made by the Crown Prosecution Service is on the condition
that prosecution would be in the public interest. At every stage of the
criminal justice process a decision is made whether to proceed with the
case – to classify as crime, to investigate, to prosecute, to sentence. At
each stage there are exceptions – for instance, if it is deemed to be not
in the public interest to prosecute. In short, we are not all treated the
same. There are perfectly good reasons for many of these exceptions;
however, the point here is that the application of rules is seldom about
zero tolerance or about equality for all concerned. Exceptions are the
norm. If this is the case then there is some merit in the postmodern
perspective drawing on chaos theory, that disorder is in fact the normal
situation (Henry and Milovanovic, 1996). What seems to occur is
the formation of 'rules for breaking rules' (Edgerton, 1985); a sort of
'orderly disorder' (Milovanovic, 1997).

The normative view of rules and rule adherence is that the 'normal'
position is for people to follow society's moral and legal rules and make
these rules part of who they are. However, it is possible that what is
'normal' is in fact the reverse; that it is normal to find exceptions to rules
or to bend or break rules; and the 'deviant' act is to actually follow all

of society's rules and laws. Rules are situationally interpreted; as James Lull notes, 'Every use of a rule is an interpretation of a rule' (2000: 87). They are also bent or broken to suit the situation. As noted previously, we are all law breakers. In an era of late modern individualism it is also possible that we all bend rules or find exceptions to suit our own personal advantage.

In 1969 the sociologist Erving Goffman considered what he called strategic interaction. Goffman is probably best known for his work on symbolic interaction, how there is an element of theatre to face-to-face encounters, and that different social rules exist for different types of encounter depending on familiarity with others and the size of the gathering (1963). For strategic interaction the focus is on the game-like qualities of interactions, where the objective is to maximise personal advantage, an idea that has since evolved into game theory (Swedberg, 2001). Gaming is certainly evident in economics and business, and to a certain extent in many everyday interactions. However, according to Robert Edgerton (1985) such strategic interaction only tells part of the story. While each of us can be strategic, other rules are followed: 'Our proverb that "rules are made to be broken" is only a part of social reality, the part comprehended by strategic interaction ideas. Other rules are made to be followed, and they are followed, usually, even when it is difficult to do so' (Edgerton, 1985: 260).

While we can bend rules, find exceptions to rules, or clearly breach rules set before us, there are a lot of rules and laws that we do follow. If we did not, then any kind of ordered social existence would be very difficult. But even when bending or breaking rules, it is possible that we are following different, alternative sets of rules that just contradict the norm. For example, the urban criminologist Alison Young has described city living as various 'cities within the city' (2014: 48). The same urban spaces accommodate different people with differing and sometimes conflicting understandings of urban existence. At the surface there is the 'legislated city' where those with power dictate which behaviours are acceptable. Below this there are various 'uncommissioned cities' occupied by those with different ways of interacting with other people and with the city. Conflict and criminalisation occur when these plural 'cities' interact. For instance, a parcour runner or street artist would have a very different understanding of urban space to someone out shopping. Someone enjoying the night-time economy may use the city quite differently to the manager of a corporation on a business trip. Each version of the city develops its own normative rules. So while each may be breaking or bending the rules of the legislated city they may also be adhering to their own rules and normative standards. The key for successful urban cosmopolitanism will be when each version of the city recognises and appreciates other ways of living as well as their impact on others (See also Millie, 2009c; 2016).

Conclusions

While politicians are keen for us to 'play by the rules', this chapter has questioned what this actually means in contemporary Western capitalist society. It is apparent that playing by the rules is not so straightforward and that the rules of society are often bent or broken for personal gain, and exceptions to rules are common. One way to encourage playing by the rules is through a social contract. According to Hobbes, cooperative action can only be encouraged through self-interest; and at a time when individualism is a dominant force he may have a point. However, this view overlooks the altruism and empathy that do still exist, drawing on Golden Rule ideas of reciprocity and even perhaps the Christian 'economy of gift and its logic of superabundance' (Ricoeur, 1990: 395). While self-interest may dominate, it cannot explain all actions and omissions. Thus ideas of social contract do not have to be based entirely on self-interest, although of course allowing for self-interest may make broader compliance more likely.

The chapter has highlighted problems with a social contract based on democratic government. While it might be the best option available, it is possible that those elected will ignore the general will of the people, or might intervene too much in each of our lives. There is a risk that social control may take precedence over meaningful contract between citizen and state. Rules are then enforced rather than negotiated. If the government is to reflect the majority, there are also issues if this majority is parochial in outlook, or simply prejudiced. The minority are thereby further marginalised.

Another consideration for this chapter has been whether it is always right to adhere to society's normative and legal rules. If rules are prejudicial or discriminatory then the morally right thing to do might be to break such rules. Politicians often talk of rights and responsibilities; yet, according to Dworkin (1977), rights trump non-rights objectives, even if these are in law. Examples given in this chapter included the assistance of fugitive slaves in 19th-century America, or aiding Jews in Nazi Germany. In both instances the morally right thing is to break the law. Such a view is opposite to Socrates' contention that it is right to comply with society's laws, even if these are bad laws. Rather, non-compliance and civil disobedience may be morally right, otherwise the rules of society will never be challenged. It is contended that such challenge ought to be in a way that demonstrates respect for others (see Chapter Seven). Here Kant's emphasis on duty is relevant, that we have a duty to respect the moral law, which is not the same as blindly following the laws and rules laid down by the state. The chapter highlighted that society's normative and legal rules are human made and are therefore imperfect. As such, the law cannot, by definition, be absolutely good. The possibility of natural or moral law was considered, as reflected in the Golden Rule. It was argued that there are basic or natural laws, that some basic goods are always good. Yet, beyond this is the law as written where there is room for interpretation. Using the example of murder, it is generally agreed that this is a moral 'bad'; however, even here there is interpretation with various forms of manslaughter, justifiable homicide and killing during wartime, and so on. In short, there are exceptions to the basic moral law on murder (Edgerton, 1985). Jeremy Bentham was sceptical of the idea of natural rights. More recent legal positivists have been equally critical of the notion of natural law and rights. Drawing on Dworkin (1977), the chapter has taken a view that society's laws are at least based on some form of morality, even if this is sometimes mistaken. While there are natural laws and generally agreed moral principles, it is not always clear how they are played out in everyday use of rules and laws.

The law itself operates through a system of exceptions and is not equally applied in all situations. Not only are there accepted exceptions to rules and laws, they can also be bent to suit the situation. It is possible that exceptions are so common and rules are so frequently bent that the deviant act would be to strictly follow society's rules and laws. Here game theory may be relevant, in that rules are used to suit individual advantage, or to benefit certain connections. With rules unequally applied there is potential for conflict. The key to minimise such conflict, and a possible positive way forward, is a focus on respect for other positions and this is considered in the chapter that follows.

Notes

[1] Bruce Cockburn, 'The Trouble with Normal' (1983).

SEVEN

Respect

Introduction

So far this book has considered philosophical ideas of values, morality, aesthetics, order and rules and how they relate to criminological concern. This chapter explores a positive way forward centred on the concept of respect. The meaning of 'respect' has been a concern for moral philosophy for some time (for example Darwall, 1977; Dworkin, 1977; Hill, 2000; Bagnoli, 2007; Carter, 2011). Much of this work draws, at least in part, on the writings of Immanuel Kant centred on the categorical imperative (see Chapter Three) and the notion of human dignity, that 'respect for the moral law entails treating persons (oneself included) always as ends in themselves and never simply as means' (Darwall, 1977: 36). In effect, human dignity prescribes that people should never be considered means to an end. According to Thomas Hill (2000: 69), a Kantian perspective is that 'human beings are to be regarded as worthy of respect as human beings, regardless of how their values differ and whether or not we disapprove of what they do'. In this way respect is due to all persons, regardless of who they are. Such egalitarianism has been problematic for some. For instance, according to Stephen Darwall (1977: 37):

> The claim that all persons are entitled to respect just by virtue of being persons may not seem wholly unproblematic, however. How could respect be something which is due to all persons? Do we not also think that persons can either deserve or fail to deserve our respect? Is the moralist who claims that all persons are entitled to respect advocating that we give up this idea?

This chapter unpicks the meaning of respect and whether respect for all can work alongside respect having to be earned. Drawing on Kantian philosophy, and work by Stephen Darwall (1977) and Thomas Hill (2000) in particular, two types of respect are outlined. The political use of the language of respect is then considered in the context of work on mutuality. Respect for self is regarded as just as important as respect for others. The chapter also considers the place of deference. It is concluded that if those with power in society want respect, they must simply first show respect, but not demand it in return. This is not how politicians have regarded respect, and such an approach would be a challenge for criminal justice agencies.

Politics and two types of respect

Stephen Darwall (1977) conceived of respect as being either recognition respect or appraisal respect. Recognition respect acknowledges that people are 'entitled to have other persons take seriously and weigh appropriately the fact that they are persons in deliberating about what they do' (1977: 38). This clearly draws on the notion of human dignity and Kant's ideas concerning persons as ends and not means. According to Darwall, the alternative is 'appraisal respect' where respect has to be earned, 'persons or features which are held to manifest their excellence as persons or as engaged in some specific pursuit' (1977: 38). This relates to ideas of esteem and merit; as Darwall noted: '... when we speak of someone as meriting or deserving our respect, it is appraisal respect that we have in mind' (1977: 39).

Examples would be a sports person or musician earning our respect, or work colleague being the best that they can be. Despite their apparent contradictions, both recognition and appraisal respect often work together, recognising that all persons have inherent dignity and ought to be equally respected, but also that how we live our lives, through thought, word and action, can generate praise from others, that we earn respect or disrespect. The narratives used by politicians employ both forms of respect. Of relevance to criminology, where the emphasis lies has an impact on how society views and treats others who are unlike ourselves.

Politicians are keen to tell us that we need to show respect. Just as divides are presented between law abiders and law breakers (see previous chapter), a clear division can be presented between a respectful us, and disrespectful others. In 2005 Tony Blair as British Prime Minister announced his intention to encourage a society characterised by 'respect'. While the notion of respect can apply to all aspects of our lives, Blair's project was focused on antisocial behaviour (Millie, 2009a; 2009b). A Home Office-led 'Respect Task Force' was created, followed by a 'Respect Action Plan' in January 2006. In launching the Respect Task Force Tony Blair stated that 'We will take tough action so that the majority of law-abiding, decent people no longer have to tolerate the behaviour of the few individuals and families that think they do not have to show respect to others' (Respect Task Force, 2006: 1).

As discussed previously, just as we are all law breakers, it is unlikely that there is a neat divide between those that are respectful and disrespectful. That said, a dichotomy between a good 'us' and a bad 'them' is a convenient narrative to sell to an electorate keen to believe the myth of the law-abiding majority. Blair was aware that such a narrative could have a labelling effect. To defend his position he claimed: 'We are not demonising them. We are simply asking that the local community can get to have the power to make these people conform or face the consequences' (BBC News Online, 2007). His view of 'conform or face the consequences' made uncomfortable reading (Millie, 2009b). The language of respect here was clearly divisive. It was respect on his terms and it had to be earned. In line with Darwall (1977) it can be regarded as a form of 'appraisal respect'. Blair had taken some inspiration from the sociologist Richard Sennett (2003), although Sennett was less complementary about Blair's respect agenda in stating, 'Is it any surprise to you that a politician who elicits less and less respect from his public thinks that the public has a problem with respect' (Sennett, 2006). For Sennett, rather than focusing on people's antisocial behaviour, attention ought to have been on how institutions could be better behaved.

In this context Blair's understanding of respect was that it needed to be earned; yet elsewhere he has talked of respect being due to all persons, of 'recognition respect'. For instance, in 2001 he outlined his political values stating that 'Our values are clear. The equal worth of all citizens, and their right to be treated with equal respect and consideration despite their differences, are fundamental. So too is individual responsibility.'

The idea of rights and responsibilities was central to Blair's supposed 'third way' approach to politics (Giddens, 1998); but there is potential tension between respect being due to all persons (our rights) and respect having to be earned (our responsibilities). This tension is also apparent in the language used by the former Conservative Prime Minister David Cameron. For instance, demonstrating that respect should be earned Cameron stated, following the 2011 urban riots in England, that 'This is not about poverty, it's about culture. A culture that glorifies violence, shows disrespect to authority, and says everything about rights but nothing about responsibilities' (Cameron 2011).

Yet, elsewhere in a speech concerning British business with China, Cameron talked in terms of recognition respect, that 'My Government is committed to working with the Chinese government in a way of mutual respect and understanding to deepen these relations and remove barriers to trade and investment and partnership between our two countries' (Cameron, 2013).

In his post-Prime Ministerial life, Tony Blair continued to talk about respect, but his emphasis shifted to international issues with the Tony Blair Faith Foundation established 'to build respect and understanding between and about the major religions'.[1] It was a theme picked up by the US President Barak Obama in a 2012 speech at Cairo University, in which he stated that his aim was to 'seek a new beginning between the United States and Muslims around the world, one based on mutual interest and mutual respect'. In political use of the term, 'respect' is related to how we get on with one another, from everyday encounters and perceived antisocial behaviour, through to relations with other religions or other global markets and cultures. Respect is due to all persons; but then it also has to be earned.

Mutual respect

According to Richard Sennett (2003) the notion of mutuality is central to respect. Mutuality moves respect away from Kant's egalitarianism and recognition respect. Rather, respect is something that is performed needing reciprocity between all parties. Sennett observed that 'mutuality requires expressive work. It must be enacted, performed' (2003: 59). Respect is not passive but earned by actively taking part in the performance and by respecting the other players. Sennett expanded a musical analogy recalling playing in an orchestra: 'When I first began to play chamber music, my teacher ordered me to respect the other players without, again, explaining what she meant. But musicians learn to do so, usually by using their ears rather than words' (Sennett, 2003: 50). Without this mutual respect there would be musical chaos. Sennett admitted that translating this to the social world is not an easy task: 'an enormous gap exists between wanting to act well toward others and doing so' (2003: 59).

Sennett emphasised respect being earned through having a talent or learning to work with others. His perspective on mutuality is similar to Jane Jacobs' (1961/1992) romantic view of a working city street, as previously outlined in Chapter Five. For Jacobs a successful city street can be likened to a dance: 'an intricate ballet in which the individual dancers and ensembles all have distinctive parts which miraculously reinforce each other' (1961/1992: 50). As previously noted, problems exist when those living in the city are performing separate dances that conflict with one other. To stretch Sennett's analogy, there are problems when some musicians prefer to play hip hop, or punk, or any other form of music, rather than chamber music. If this is the case, how is mutual respect possible if the musicians want to play fundamentally different styles of music (or in Jacobs' case, perform different dances)? According to Carla Bagnoli (2007) understanding that others have an equal standing obliges us to enter into dialogue with them, but it does not mean we have to agree: 'We can respectfully disagree. In fact, respect requires that we do not impose our views on others, but it also requires that we engage in a frank dialogue with them. ... The conclusion of this dialogue may be informed disagreement' (Bagnoli, 2007: 117).

True mutuality can coexist with disagreement and, to continue Sennett's analogy, it recognises others' musical styles (and other dances). Translating this to how we ought to live together respectfully it is worth returning to Alison Young's (2014) concept of 'cities within the city' as considered in Chapter Six (see also Millie, 2016). The idea is that the same urban space has to accommodate different visions of city living, that in effect there are different cities overlaying the official 'legislated city'. Respect is only possible if these different ways of living (or dances, or styles of music) are mutually recognised.

It is the 'bridging social capital' between strangers that Robert Putnam (2000) advocates. It is also a cosmopolitan approach, which, according to Ulf Hannerz (1990: 103), can be regarded as 'an orientation, a willingness to engage with the Other'. One does not have to agree with the Other, but has to at least be willing to engage. Leonie Sandercock (2003: 2) further describes a utopian 'Cosmopolis' characterised by '... genuine acceptance of, connection with, and respect and space for the cultural other, and ... the possibility of a togetherness in difference'.

The idea of 'togetherness in difference' is key; yet, as Peter Squires notes, 'Deep mutual respect is a scarce resource and it evaporates quickly in the heat of competitive exchange, even among supposed equals' (2009: 242). Furthermore, late modern city living can lead to individualism and isolation rather than cosmopolitanism, thus making mutual recognition, engagement and respect all the more difficult. For instance, according to Anthony Giddens:

> Personal meaningless – the feeling that life has nothing worthwhile to offer – becomes a fundamental psychic problem in circumstances of late modernity ... 'Existential isolation' is not so much a separation of individuals from

others as a separation from the moral resources necessary
to live a full and satisfying existence. (Giddens, 1991: 9)

With people often living parallel individualised lives, or retreating into
isolated existences, any project to engender greater mutual respect is
going to be difficult. However, this does not mean the promotion of
respect is not important. The journalist Lynn Truss has already been
quoted in saying that, 'all the important rules surely boil down to one:
remember you are with other people; show some consideration' (2005: 12,
emphasis in original). This is also true of respect. There perhaps ought
to be an inherent respect for each person's human dignity (a Kantian
perspective), but this does not mean abhorrent behaviour should be
respected. On the contrary, the justice system is there to intervene if
anyone uses another human as a means to an end. Mutuality may be
a useful way to understand how such degradation of dignity can be
minimised.

A further example of mutual respect is provided in a recent speech
by Australian Prime Minister Malcolm Turnbull following a terrorist
attack in Sydney in 2015 – as outlined in the previous chapter. Here
respect is translated as togetherness through mutuality. According to
Turnbull, mutual respect 'is the glue that binds this very diverse country
together'. Furthermore:

> Mutual respect is fundamental to our harmony as a
> multicultural society and it is fundamental to our success.
> It's fundamental to our future prosperity. It's fundamental to
> our national security. Now the key to that mutual respect is
> that it is a two-way street. Every religion, every faith, every
> moral doctrine understands the golden rule, 'do unto others
> as you would have them do unto you'. So if we want to be
> respected, if we want our faith, our cultural background
> to be respected, then we have to respect others. That is a
> fundamental part of the Australian project. (Turnbull, on
> ABC News, 2015a)

Of course, Turnbull may not always display such mutual respect, and
he was painting an optimistic picture of Australian life; but perhaps
optimism is what is needed. Returning to Tony Blair's respect agenda,
when asked about the new politics of respect, the Archbishop of York
John Sentamu stated that 'If we expect young people to be respectful,
we should show respect. If they are not treated lovingly and forgivingly,

they will be unforgiving. If we do not trust them, they will not trust us' (2006).

Sentamu was using the language of mutuality, but unlike Blair's respect being earned on his terms, it has more in common with Turnbull's perspective, that if we want to be respected we must first show respect. It leads by example. It is hopeful to achieve reciprocity but does not demand it. This is equal to the Christian 'economy of gift' (Ricoeur, 1990), as previously noted, that we choose to treat others with love and mercy. We might hope for mutual reciprocity, but we do not necessarily expect it in return. Such an approach is not unique to Christian theology and is something that criminal justice agencies could learn from. Research within social psychology and criminology on procedural justice (for example Alexander and Ruderman, 1987; Lind and Tyler, 1988; Hough et al, 2010) indicates that organisations – and especially criminal justice agencies – are regarded by the public as having greater legitimacy if they are seen to be fair; and that 'fair procedures can act to reduce generally the level of conflict and dispute' (Lind and Tyler, 1988: 82). Agencies such as the police can lead by example in demonstrating respect for all that they come in contact with. An officer does not have to agree with a person's perspective, and does not have to approve of their behaviour, but should still recognise their inherent dignity. Such an attitude might, for example, change approaches to stop-and-search or racial/religious profiling.

Respect for self

Continuing with Christian theology, an important part of any understanding of respect is consideration of respect for self. As previously noted, Jesus highlighted the commandment to 'Love your neighbour as yourself' (Matthew 22:39). This was a repeat of the Old Testament instruction in Leviticus (19:18): 'Do not seek revenge or bear a grudge against one of your people, but love your neighbour as yourself. I am the Lord.' The suggestion is that love for self and love for others are equal and interdependent. It is possible that this is the same for self-respect and respect for others.

With late modern individualism there is a risk that respect for self will be regarded as more important than respect for others. At the very least, many people might be blind to the needs of others believing that 'it is my right to behave how I like, and for others to behave how I would expect them' (Millie, 2006: 11). Such a position is clearly disrespectful. Furthermore, there is an assortment of places where one can look for self-respect. This can be constructively through showing respect for others, or perhaps in doing a job to the best of your ability; but it can also be through involvement in activities that use others as a means to an end. For instance, gang and familial honour codes often refer to respect (for example Bourgois, 1996; Anderson, 1999; Squires 2009). For John Braithwaite (2000) the shame and disrespect that authorities sometimes show can make criminal subcultures appear all the more attractive: 'When respectable society rejects me, I have a status problem; I am in the market for a solution to this status problem. Criminal subcultures can supply that solution' (Braithwaite, 2000: 287). Furthermore, according to Braithwaite: 'Disrespect begets disrespect. Because you don't respect me, I won't respect you or the rules you value. I have no hope of seeking out a respected identity under your values; delinquent subcultures look more promising to me as a basis for respect' (2000: 287–8).

What is needed is appreciation of inherent human dignity; a form of recognition respect. As John Sentamu (2006) claimed, 'If we expect young people to be respectful, we should show respect'. A state-enforced respect agenda centred on conforming or having to face the consequences is not the best way to go about this. The result for some is that self-respect is found in what Elijah Anderson has called the code of the street: 'At the heart of the code is the issue of respect – loosely defined as being treated "right" or being granted one's "props" (or proper due) or the deference one deserves' (Anderson, 1999: 33).

The code is very much based on appraisal respect and respect being earned. The aforementioned Biblical instruction not to seek revenge or to bear a grudge would be anathema to such understandings of respect. In many ways the 'street' understanding of respect is itself disrespectful, often based on others as means to an end. Street respect is also hierarchical and based on deference.

Deference

As previously highlighted, the idea of deference is tied in with notions of social position and respect for authority. This may be within a hierarchical class system, a street gang, or a family. For instance, in talking about respect for mothers Thomas Hill (2000: 89–90) notes:

> Suppose someone says, 'She has not been a particularly good mother, but she is my mother, after all, and I must respect her as such.' … merely holding a certain position, or standing in a certain relationship to another, is sometimes enough to warrant a (presumptive) claim of respect.

As noted, over the past century there has been a demise in traditional hierarchies in society and automatic deference. The kind of social snobbery tracked by Pierre Bourdieu (1979/1984) that looks down on the tastes of lower classes has been substantially challenged. That said, automatic subordination is still expected by some with power in society. Furthermore, and as highlighted in Chapter Five, some people take comfort in knowing how they fit into the social order. Their self-respect is tied to ideas of status. However, deference is not the same as respect with humans regarded as being of unequal worth; and as Thomas Hill has highlighted (2000: 59), 'people stigmatized as inferior may still feel, quite rightly, that they "get no respect"'.

Conclusions

A common theme throughout this book has been how we get on with one another – and what happens when we do not. This chapter has focused on how we can better get on with one another and has considered respect as an overarching concept for improving social connectedness. According to Darwall (1977) there are two types of respect, these being recognition respect and appraisal respect. Recognition respect has most in common with Kant's notion that all persons should be recognised as ends, and never as means to an end. It is respect based on egalitarian dignity where all are due respect, irrespective of whether we agree with what they do (Bagnoli, 2007). Such a view would be problematic for some who instead focus on appraisal respect. Here respect has to be earned. Despite their contradictions, this chapter has taken the view that both recognition and appraisal respect can often work together.

The political appropriation of the term 'respect' can be powerful, as exemplified by Tony Blair's 2000s' 'respect agenda'. However, in this instance it was very much based on respect being earned and was on the government's terms. There was a clear divide created between a respectful 'us' and disrespectful 'them' (Millie, 2009b). Nonetheless, just as we are all law breakers, the divide between respectful and disrespectful is not likely to be neat. In talking about respect Blair also adopted the language of rights and responsibilities; but there is tension between respect being due to all (our rights) and respect being earned (our responsibilities).

Another way to consider respect is in terms of mutuality. Here Sennett (2003) has used a musical example where all the players in an orchestra have to show mutual respect in order to perform a piece to the best of their ability. That said, Sennett admitted that translating this idea to the social world is not easy. It was contended in this chapter that outside of the orchestra not only do musicians not necessarily want to play together, but they may want to play completely different styles. Alison Young's (2014) concept of 'cities within the city' is useful here to aid understanding – that the same urban space has to accommodate different understandings of city living, and that there are different versions of the city overlaying the official city. Respect is only possible if these differences are mutually recognised – albeit with the understanding that none of these versions of city living causes harm to others. Such behaviour that sees others as a means to an end is still not respected. In urban sociological terms it is the equivalent to bridging social capital or a form of cosmopolitan urbanism; as Hannerz has described: 'an orientation, a willingness to engage with the Other' (1990: 103). This is a challenge to the individualism of late modernity.

As noted, according to the Archbishop of York John Sentamu, 'If we expect young people to be respectful, we should show respect' (2006). It is a choice to treat people with respect. Drawing on the Christian 'economy of gift' (Ricoeur, 1990), such a perspective is hopeful of reciprocity, but does not demand it. Criminal justice agencies can learn from such a view of respect. Drawing on work on procedural justice, by treating everyone fairly and recognising all with respect (despite what they may be accused of), the police and other agencies may gain greater legitimacy and respect from those they encounter. Such a change of emphasis may also impact approaches to stop-and-search, racial/religious profiling or other areas of criminal justice work where certain sectors of society are disproportionately targeted.

The chapter has also considered the role for self-respect, seeing it as equally valuable as respect for others. Yet, with late modern individualism some may see respect for them, or their rights, as trumping respect and rights for others. Also, some may seek respect through criminal gang subculture that, in itself, is disrespectful of others. As Braithwaite (2000) has highlighted, if authorities do not show people respect, then such criminal subcultures become more attractive – 'disrespect begets disrespect'. In line with John Sentamu's ideas of being first to show respect, and Kant's notion of human dignity being due to all, perhaps such gangs will be less attractive in the first place. The chapter finished by considering the place of deference. Respect is not the same as deference where we are expected to show respect for authority. If those with power in society want respect, they must simply first show respect – but not demand it in return.

Notes

[1]   See https://secure.thebiggive.org.uk/charity/view/9444/the-tony-blair-faith-foundation.

EIGHT

Conclusions

Introduction

Both criminology and philosophy share concerns about how we might get on with one another and what we could, or perhaps ought to do when we do not. In this concluding chapter the place of a philosophical criminology is considered. According to Christopher Williams and Bruce Arrigo:

> Historically, philosophers have written very little about the subject of crime. Similarly, criminologists have written very little about the subject of philosophy. In both cases, the linkages between philosophy and crime have been left implicit ... However, to be sure, law and justice have been particularly significant concerns throughout the history of philosophy. (Williams and Arrigo, 2006: 1)

As highlighted in the introduction to this book, criminology is an interdisciplinary enterprise and, as such, it makes sense for criminologists to engage with other disciplines such as philosophy that have for centuries attempted to answer questions of importance to criminology. Williams and Arrigo (2006) are right to say that there has been little engagement between philosophy and criminology; as they go on to observe, 'since its modern inception criminology has not been a discipline of systematic philosophical debate, analysis, or critique' (2006: 15). This book has been an attempt to engender greater engagement between the two subject areas. There is much within philosophy of direct relevance to criminological enquiry. Similarly, philosophy might gain from associating with a subject so closely related to people's everyday lived realities. By engaging with philosophy this book has demonstrated that textbook histories of criminological thought only present a partial picture of ideas central to criminological understanding.

This concluding chapter reflects on the previous seven chapters and assesses the usefulness of a philosophical approach to criminology. As highlighted in the introduction, both philosophy and criminology are broad subject areas and, as such, this book has been selective in terms of topics covered. Rather than attempt to cover everything within philosophy that is of relevance to criminology, it has instead focused on six areas regarded as important for criminological understanding; these being value judgements, morality, aesthetics, order/disorder, rules and respect.

But first the book considered what criminology is actually about. Criminology was compared to post-Duchamp modern and contemporary art – that criminology has become whatever we want it to be and an academic 'does' criminology if that is how they label their work. In short, I call myself a criminologist, therefore what I do is criminology. This is not a particularly helpful position for any subject. In effect, criminology becomes a sort of 'bad-ology', or the study of anything we happen to find objectionable including crime, deviance, harm, non-normative behaviour, incivility, morally repugnant or offensive behaviour, or whatever we define as wrong or simply bad. If David Garland (2011) was right in saying that criminology lacks a unifying epistemology, perhaps it also lacks a unifying subject of study beyond simply being the study of the 'bad stuff that happens'. The position taken in this book has been that the core of criminology remains 'crime' – despite crime itself lacking an ontological reality (that said, the same could be also said for social harm or deviance, for example). The criminologist can then move away from this core to investigate other related areas of interest, such as harms, deviance, incivility or non-normative behaviour. As noted, Stanley Cohen (1988: 9) was of the view that criminology's task is to consider: 'Why are laws made? Why are they broken? What do we do or what should we do about this?' Not all criminologists would agree with such an assessment or indeed the methods used to answer such questions. There has been a Balkanisation within the subject with a degree of intolerance of other positions, be they those of crime scientists or experimental criminologists, or cultural, critical or ultra-realist criminologists, or somewhere in between. A similar divide is evident within philosophy between analytic and continental traditions, which, at their extremes, risk scientism on the one hand, and obscurantism on the other (see for example Critchley, 2001). Rather than seeing one particular brand of criminology as the only way forward, this book has favoured the kind of open dialogue and debate that allows for greatest knowledge and understanding of the subject through engagement with others across criminology, and with others in different academic disciplines – including philosophy. It recognises the value of scientific enquiry, but not the idea that scientific method is applicable to all situations or can answer all questions. Furthermore, such scientific enquiry needs to acknowledge the subjectivity of crime. Just as science is not well equipped to answer existential questions, non-scientific approaches to criminology will be better placed to consider questions regarding the meaning and subjective experience of crime, harm and deviance. It is acknowledged that, while it is easy to present a picture of divides, many philosophers (and criminologists) work somewhere between such extremes. Similarly, this book has drawn from both continental and analytic traditions and from those in between.

Context and power have been recognised as key determinates for what and who become criminalised, and both have been considered throughout this book. There has been particular emphasis on Kantian philosophy, especially regarding human dignity. Relatedly the book has drawn on ideas concerning the Golden Rule and Paul Ricoeur's (1990) work on Christian theology and an 'economy of gift' (see, for instance, Chapter Three). In this concluding chapter each of the preceding chapters is looked at in turn. Building on the common themes of dignity, respect and the economy of gift, the possibility of an empathetic criminology is considered. The chapter concludes by reflecting on the merits of a philosophical criminology.

Values

In Chapter Two it was highlighted that value-neutral research is not possible, despite some academics' claims to the contrary. In fact, values are critical to our judgements of good and bad, and what actions or omissions are celebrated, tolerated or censured. A relativist would argue that what is valued as good or bad in one culture might well be different elsewhere. Such difference is acknowledged and there is clearly a plurality of beliefs and values within cultures, let alone across different cultural groups. However, a purely relativist position was discounted as this, in theory, would be tolerant of behaviours that are generally regarded as intolerable. For instance, a group's moral values may allow for torture, rape, slavery or genocide. Just because, from their perspective, these are the right things to be doing does not mean they are correct in that assessment. Based on Kantian notions of inherent human dignity, such activities should *always* be wrong, no matter what. So, rather than a relativist view, in Chapter Two it was contended that there are some universal moral values that ought to be applicable to all and that some things are always wrong. Yet below this there is room for interpretation and perception.

An important consideration is whose values are regarded as most important in society. In the late modern capitalist West there are certain groups or individuals that have greater power in dictating the values we follow. Drawing on Becker (1963) these include politicians, the media and various 'moral entrepreneurs'. In a democracy there is also majoritarian influence, although the extent to which majority values are followed might not be as strong as suspected. There are also powerful multinational corporations and other agencies with influence that dictate how we live.

The relevance of value judgements to criminology is regarding questions of criminalisation. As Anthony Duff (2010) has observed, there is currently a crisis of criminalisation with behaviours that are regarded as risky or outside the norm too readily censured. An appreciation of values helps us to understand why certain actions or omissions are criminalised, tolerated or celebrated. It also helps with understanding why something may be regarded as wrong in one situation but accepted or tolerated in another.

Four types of value judgement were considered, these being moral, aesthetic, prudential and economic value judgements. In late modern capitalist societies economic value judgements can dominate. Alternatively, prudential or quality-of-life concerns may be regarded as important – as with Bill Bratton's (1995) famous emphasis on quality-of-life policing. Aesthetic value judgements can dictate whether something or someone is regarded as appropriate for an approved aesthetic. If not, then they may be moved on, or worse. Moral value judgements are also clearly important in determining what and who are regarded as acceptable, tolerable or censurable, and in what contexts. Morals were considered in more detail in Chapter Three.

Morals

According to Anthony Bottoms (2002: 24), 'all criminologists have to be interested in morality' as many criminological concerns are also moral concerns, such as decisions to criminalise, how to police, and whether and how to punish. There is clearly significant crossover between moral philosophy and criminology. In Chapter Three various moral issues were considered, including the merits of focusing on virtues and character, theories of obligation and various consequentialist and deontological approaches. The limitations for criminology of ethical egoism and utilitarianism were highlighted. For instance, according to Stanley Cohen (1998) criminology has been concerned with maximising utility; but as Cohen notes, the ends do not always justify the means. This is an important observation for criminology and puts moral limits on the use of social control, intrusive investigation, dishonest practices or disproportionate punishment. It was highlighted that criminology is on the side of the oppressed, the 'other'. As such, majoritarian conceptions of utility are also problematic. By maximising the utility of the majority we may also be diminishing the importance of the minority.

The Golden Rule was highlighted as a potentially useful way of understanding morality, to 'do to others what you would have them do to you' (Matthew 7:12). More specifically, Kant's categorical imperative is a useful place to start in order to understand why certain actions or omissions ought to be regarded as morally wrong and, maybe, censurable. Unlike utilitarianism, the categorical imperative is non-consequentialist, but focuses on whether actions conform to a 'moral law': to 'Act only according to that maxim whereby you can at the same time will that it should become a universal law' (1785/1990: 1031). For instance, minorities should not be disproportionately targeted by the police as this action ought not become a universal law applicable to everyone. Similarly, theft could not become a universal law applied to everyone. In other words, the thief would not wish to be stolen from, or the police officer would not wish to receive the same disproportionate targeting. A key to Kant's moral philosophy is his notion of human dignity and of treating humans as ends and not means to an end, a theme I shall return to in this concluding chapter. Such a focus would be a serious challenge for criminal justice professionals. It was suggested that an even more radical challenge would be the Christian economy of gift and logic of superabundance (Ricoeur, 1990). Here reciprocity may be hoped for, but it is not demanded. This was considered further in Chapter Seven on respect. According to Ricoeur, it was perhaps the intention of the Golden Rule in the first place.

Aesthetics

Chapter Four focused on aesthetics and criminology. It was demonstrated that aesthetic expectations can also determine what is acceptable, tolerable or censurable behaviour. The example of a graffiti writer or street artist was used where the aesthetic expectations in one district may result in their activities being celebrated. Elsewhere people may be less receptive to their graffiti or street art with calls for censure and possible imprisonment. As with earlier consideration of values and morals, the tastes and preferences of the powerful have tended to dictate what is regarded as aesthetically acceptable. Aesthetic tastes have a lot to do with economic value. For instance, the value of work by the street artist Banksy – both direct value and potential value in attracting tourists to an area – has been a consideration in deciding whether a piece should stay or be removed (Millie, 2008). The potential value to the community is also a concern (Hansen, 2015). Away from the urban landscape, ideas of landscape beauty can also influence the criminalisation of people or things that do not adhere to an idealised rural idyll. In this regard, aesthetics could be very important for criminology in a number of contexts. For instance, shopping centre managers can remove those that do not look like the right sort of shoppers; Gypsies, Roma and Travellers are moved on as they are deemed to be unsightly; and a multibillionaire can build a golf course, despite it being on protected land.

Aesthetics was seen as traditionally associated with beauty in arts and landscape appreciation. Yet, in line with Yuriko Saito (2007), everyday aesthetic experiences are regarded as just as important – especially when considering the relevance of aesthetics for criminology. An example given was the aesthetics of street drinking, with certain street drinkers censured, while others that contribute to the perceived vitality of the street, encouraged.

Some have claimed that an objective measure of beauty is possible. In line with a Kantian conception of beauty, a view was taken that tastes are subjective. Thus, something is aesthetically pleasing or beautiful because that is how we perceive it. As noted, the perceptions of the powerful are important in determining acceptability, and various examples were given – from the removal of entire villages by 'Capability' Brown, to the banning of hoodies within certain shopping centres. Aesthetic concerns can also clearly be criminological.

Building on the recent expansion of visual criminology an aesthetic criminology was suggested with a focus on the regulation of tastes. It would also be concerned with emotion and our affective responses to sensory encounters. Semiotics would be a useful tool for understanding how such sensory encounters are read; and in a criminological sense, whether they are read as something to be celebrated, tolerated or censured, or whether something to fear or embrace. We form bonds with certain places or settings through what Bachelard (1969) calls a love of place, or Tuan (1974) terms 'topophilia'. An aesthetic criminology would be interested in such bonds and how they are affected by experiences of crime, deviance or social harm, or perhaps by social control and the criminal justice system. A further concern for aesthetic criminology might be people who subvert our aesthetic expectations, including urban interventionists who challenge aesthetic norms, the regulation of taste and concepts of order.

Order

The ethical egoism of late modernity was summarised in a quote from Bart Simpson, that it is "My bubble, my rules". Despite Bart's claims, we do not live in isolation. The challenge is how such individualism can be married with the need for people to live together. Key to this is the creation of an acceptable social order. Criminology is, by definition, interested in notions of order and disorder. Various ordering devices are created, including the classification of people as law abiders and law breakers; although, as noted, such distinctions are not always as clear as assumed. In this instance, very few of us could genuinely be regarded as absolute law abiders. Criminological understanding of order and disorder has been influenced by Durkheim's anomie, which highlighted the disorder associated with periods of change. According to Durkheim, such disorder or associated crime comes as part of finding new ways of living and, as such, is normal in society.

While 'normal', such disorders and crimes may also be associated with harmful effects. The biblical instruction to 'Love your neighbour as yourself' was suggested as a useful consideration when attempting to reconcile the need for change and the impact this change might have on others. During periods of social change common conceptions of order are going to be challenged, but this is not a problem so long as these changes do not negatively impact on others. Drawing on Kant, others should never be regarded as means to an end.

Some people favour a strictly ordered existence. Examples included the visual need for neat rows of vegetables, or the beauty of mathematic predictability. Problems arise when demands for a neatly ordered existence dictate to others how to live their lives. The chapter also considered postmodern philosophical perspectives on catastrophe and chaos. It was suggested that chaos might in fact represent the status quo, what Milovanovic (1997) called an 'orderly disorder'. In short, what is perceived as disorderly may represent an alternative order. Again, it is a question of who gets to define what is orderly and disorderly; and again, the powerful have the biggest say. Nonetheless, some form of order is necessary for social relations to operate. For instance, there needs to be at least a form of order for coordination so that meetings happen at the right time and location, or cars do not crash into each other on the motorway. While there need to be generally accepted standards for many areas of life, there is still the possibility of alternative conceptions of order to challenge the status quo.

Social contract theory would be familiar to most criminologists. This was suggested as a way to engender greater cooperative action and to make order more likely, an idea explored further in the following chapter on rules. Also considered was the maintenance of order in capitalist economic markets, which were assumed to self-regulate through the emergence of 'spontaneous order'. This was perhaps disproved with the recent economic crisis. The self-interest that drives markets was shown to have its limitations, with state intervention needed to restore order.

The maintenance of order was highlighted as a function of the police. Yet, drawing on Ericson (1982), this was regarded as a conservative function often protecting the status quo. Perhaps the status quo needs to be questioned and new forms of order considered. An area of philosophy where notions of order are being questioned is in aesthetics. As previously highlighted, aesthetic regulation can dictate a preferred look and feel to an urban or rural landscape. This is not necessarily a bad thing; but, again at issue is who decides what an acceptable aesthetic order is.

Rules

In Chapter Six the political rhetoric of 'playing by the rules' was highlighted, although what this actually means is less certain when rules are frequently bent or broken for personal gain, as well as exceptions found to many rules – including by politicians. The social contract between state and citizens is a clear structure to engender greater adherence to society's rules. For Hobbes, self-interest should be behind such attempts at cooperation. It was highlighted that, while this may encourage greater compliance, it overlooks the possibility of altruism and empathy, notions that are explored further towards the end of this concluding chapter. It was argued that the social contract does not have to be all about self-interest – although such an emphasis may get more to pay greater attention to society's various normative and legal rules.

There are issues with social contract theory based on democratic government. Those elected may ignore the general will of the people, and there is often little opportunity to vote for someone else until the next election four to five years later. Furthermore, governments have tended to favour social control rather than a meaningful contract between state and citizen. And there is a risk that the electorate themselves may hold prejudicial or parochial views that they wish their government to reflect.

The social contract assumes that the right thing to do is to adhere to society's various rules. According to Dworkin (1977) this is not always the case, stating that rights trump non-rights objectives, even if these are written in law. Examples were given of assisting fugitive slaves, or helping Jews in Nazi Germany. Sometimes the morally right thing to do is to break society's rules – even to break the law – through non-compliance or civil disobedience. Again, drawing on Kant, challenges to law ought to be conducted in a way that demonstrates respect for others. A Kantian perspective would be that our duty is to respect the moral law, which is different to unthinkingly adhering to the laws dictated by the state.

Drawing on the Golden Rule, the possibility of moral or natural law was considered. As already noted, based on a Kantian conception of human dignity – including his imperative that humans should never be used as means to an end – the view was taken that some basic 'goods' are always good or right, and conversely some 'bads' are always bad or wrong, irrespective of what normative and legal rules dictate. Yet, beyond this, things are not so clear cut. This is not the view of legal positivism, which emphasises that all laws and normative rules are human made and therefore imperfect (and as they are imperfect, laws cannot be absolutely 'good'). Yet the fact that rules are human made is not incompatible with the possibility of the existence of natural laws. Society's rules are often based – at least in part – on an underlying morality, even if this interpretation of morality is misguided.

To demonstrate the imperfect nature of the law, it is required to operate through a system of exceptions. Furthermore, those with knowledge of the law will find it easier to find exceptions to suit their circumstances. The law can also be bent to suit the situation. It may be the case that the law and normative rules are so flexible that strict adherence becomes the deviant act. Game theory was suggested as a way to understand how rules may be treated for personal benefit. Resultant inequality in how laws are applied may possibly lead to conflict. It was suggested that a possible way to minimise such conflict is a focus on respect, as considered in the penultimate chapter.

Respect

In Chapter Seven it was suggested that respect could become an overarching concept for improving social connectedness. This is despite the political (mis)use of the language of respect, and the dominant individualism of late modernity. Two types of respect were highlighted. Drawing on Kantianism the first was recognition respect based on notions of egalitarian dignity. The second was appraisal respect based on the idea that respect has to be earned. Despite their contradictions, it was contended that both recognition and appraisal respect can work together.

Politicians have been keen to call for respect from citizens, but this has been respect on their terms and has to be earned. Tony Blair's 'respect agenda' was a clear example of such a perspective. A neat divide was created between those that are respectful and respected, and those that are disrespectful and disrespected – in a similar way that the mythical law-abiding majority is separated from law breakers. Just as we are all law breakers to varying degrees, such a neat divide between respectful and disrespectful is unlikely.

Blair drew some inspiration from the sociologist Richard Sennett (2003), although not his precise ideas. Sennett emphasised mutuality of respect using the example of players in an orchestra having to respect the other musicians. This makes for a neat analogy; but it was contended in this chapter that the reality of late modern living is that, outside of the orchestra, musicians may not wish to play together, let alone in the same musical style. Cities have to accommodate such different understandings of city living, with different visions overlapping one another. Respect may be possible if these differences are mutually recognised, so long as none of these causes harm to others, or sees others as a means to an end. What is needed is the sort of bridging social capital advocated by Putnam (2000), a form of cosmopolitan urbanism where we are willing to 'engage with the Other' (Hannerz 1990: 103).

A possible way to take ideas of respect forward is to consider the Christian 'economy of gift' (Ricoeur, 1990). This is hopeful of reciprocity, but does not demand it. Also considered was the role for self-respect, which is equal to respect for others. In late modernity, individualism may make calls to 'respect me' louder than calls to respect others. Furthermore, some people look for respect in all the wrong places, including within criminal gangs. Yet, as Braithwaite (2000) once noted, if people are not shown respect by authorities, than the respect given by membership of a criminal subculture may seem more attractive. In line with the economy of gift, we must first show respect without demanding it in return. Instead, drawing on ideas of deference, citizens are often called to show their respect for authority without those with power necessarily respecting their citizens.

An empathetic criminology

Building on Kant's emphasis on human dignity, and the Christian economy of gift, an empathetic criminology is suggested. According to Nigel Thrift (2005: 140), there is 'a misanthropic thread that runs through the modern city, a distrust and avoidance'. Late modern individualism appears to prioritise respect for self over respect for others. Yet, an empathetic understanding of respect and criminal justice is a possibility. This would also relate to August Comte's (1891) concept of altruism – described by Niall Scott and Jonathan Seglow (2007: 15) as 'benevolent and sympathetic feelings that ... ought to be promoted in place of more selfish ones'. Altruism is in effect the opposite of egoism and emphasises the promotion of others' interests.

An empathetic approach is concerned with seeing things from the others' point of view. Empathy is a popular area among certain social psychologists and cognitive neuroscientists (for example Davis, 1994; Zaki and Ochsner, 2012) in trying to find the mental processes and neural circuits responsible for emotion. In this regard empathy is related to the study of pro-social behaviours. However, according to Julinna Oxley (2011) empathy is not itself an emotion. Instead it is an experience or attitude towards 'sharing another's emotion' (2011: 11). In this regard one can *choose* to empathise. According to Jeremy Rifkin (2009) it is the 'social glue' holding social relations together; it is the ability to show solidarity. For US President Barak Obama, empathy is 'at the heart of my moral code' (2007: 66).

In many ways empathy is linked to the Golden Rule to 'do to others what you would have them do to you' (Matthew 7:12), and a Kantian notion of human dignity and recognition respect. In more common language, it is to 'stand in someone else's shoes'. The origins of empathy as a concept are thought to be with David Hume's (1739) ideas on sympathy in his *Treatise of Human Nature*. What he describes as sympathetic would today be thought of as empathetic. According to Hume, 'No quality of human nature is more remarkable, both in itself and in its consequences, than that propensity we have to sympathize [empathise] with others, and to receive by communication their inclinations and sentiments, however different from, or even contrary to our own' (1739: 316).

In relation to criminology, an empathetic approach would be able to see things from the others' perspective, be they victim, perpetrator, state or wider society. An empathetic criminology would start with recognition of the inherent human dignity in all social actors, that all should be respected irrespective of whether we agree with them, or with what they do. This does not mean we approve of abhorrent behaviour; nor does it mean we do not believe in justice. What it does mean is that we recognise the human-ness in all we deal with. Here, work on procedural justice (for example Lind and Tyler, 1988; Hough et al, 2010) might be useful in emphasising fair processes leading to greater legitimacy for agencies.

As an approach to the study of crime and criminals (and deviance and social harm), then empathy is a good place to start. Yet, empathy can also be biased. People tend to empathise with others that they can also relate to, such as family, friends and other people like themselves. Empathy is also easier with those present rather than those absent (Oxley, 2011). This form of 'relational empathy' has a lot in common with Putnum's (2000) bonding social capital in that it is often exclusive of others. In this regard group membership may be due to familial ties, or due to earning respect and thereby one's place in the group. Like bonding social capital, relational empathy is not in itself a bad thing, but, as Julinna Oxley has observed, it does not necessarily lead to moral thought or action: 'Empathy has the potential to enrich and strengthen moral deliberation, action and moral justification to others. But empathy is not intrinsically moral and does not always lead to moral thought or action' (2011: 4).

Relational empathy can lead to indifference, maybe even harm or criminal action towards others if this improves the position of those with whom we empathise. Rather, what is needed is a form of 'inclusive empathy' that is the opposite of exclusive, that sees respect as being due to all and is more associated with Putnum's (2000) bridging social capital that can reach out to strangers, and the kind of cosmopolitan urbanism (Hannerz, 1990) described in Chapter Seven.

Relating the idea of inclusive empathy to political agendas on respect, the state needs to show respect to all of its citizens, rather than just those it perceives as earning its respect. An empathetic state would be interested in why someone is behaving antisocially or criminally, rather than simply censuring their behaviour. It would also see the victim as an important element in any deliberations. According to Richard Sennett (2003) respect between state and citizen needs to be in both directions. It seems that the state's respect and empathy for its citizenry is sometimes lacking. As Peter Squires (2009: 260) has noted, there is 'a profound preoccupation with the "worth" of individuals at a time when some individuals appear to be "worth" less than others'.

As well as being related to Kant's notion of human dignity, an empathetic criminology might also draw inspiration from the Christian 'economy of gift'. As noted, many would be deterred by its religious associations – that because God has been generous with us we choose to be generous with others. Yet, the basic principal behind the economy of gift is not dependent on religious belief – that we treat others with love and mercy even if we do not expect it in return. It is an attitude where we lead by example simply because we are empathetic to the situation of others and want to show them the dignity they deserve. As highlighted in Chapter Three, the consequences for criminal justice agencies of such an approach would be radical, emphasising generosity, mercy and love. It would be characterised by grace, the art of giving without expecting in return.

A philosophical criminology

When I first decided to write this book I was aware that criminology – along with many other disciplines and subject areas – could be blinkered to what is going on elsewhere in the academic world. Over the past decade I have been writing about respect, values and aesthetics as they relate to criminological concerns and was drawn increasingly to philosophical writings on these subjects. It became clear that there is a great deal that criminology can learn from closer engagement with philosophy; however, the language of philosophers can be off-putting for the uninitiated. What I hope to have achieved with this book is to make some of the philosophical debates and ideas of relevance to criminology more accessible. Building on these, I have also contributed some ideas of my own.

As stated in the introduction, much of criminology is sociological, yet there is room for a philosophical criminology. The aim has not been to create another niche within criminology where those interested in philosophy can hide and do their philosophising with little impact on the rest of the subject. Badging this work as 'philosophical criminology' was always a risk. Instead, engagement with philosophy is relevant across the whole of criminology. Certainly, realisation that philosophers have been asking similar questions to criminologists for a number of centuries may mean a rethink for the chronology of the birth of criminological thought. There is certainly more to it that Lombroso, Durkheim, Bentham and Beccaria. While criminology is divided between a whole range of specialisms and approaches, so too has philosophy witnessed divides. A further aim of this book has been to draw from across these divides while, hopefully, avoiding the pitfalls of obscurantism and scientism. I make no apology for this approach as I believe knowledge and wisdom are often best found when looking outside our ontological and disciplinary bunkers.

There have been particular themes running through the book. Notably there has been frequent emphasis on Kantian philosophy, with particular prominence given to his categorical imperative and his emphases on human dignity and respect. I have also used a number of ideas from Christian theology, especially the notion of an economy of gift and logic of superabundance (Ricoeur, 1990). While social science has often turned its back on religion, I made the deliberate decision to see what could be found here. The idea of an economy of gift can be taken away from its religious roots and be used to inform an egalitarian and empathetic approach to criminal justice. This would not be easy – and the idea may be utopian – but, the basic premise is attractive: that agencies should lead by example, be empathetic to the situation of others, and want to show them the dignity they deserve.

I shall finish by re-emphasising that this book has presented 'a' philosophical criminology, and not necessarily the definitive account of philosophy and criminology. Clearly, if someone else had written the book it may have had a different emphasis or flavour – be it more analytical or perhaps with greater weight given to existentialism. Furthermore, someone else may have covered different topics entirely, perhaps with a focus on punishment and justice. I have been selective in the topics I have covered by focusing on those philosophical topics that have criminological interest, but perhaps are less often investigated. If the reader wishes to know more about, for example, the philosophy of punishment and justice then there are numerous examples of legal philosophy that will be of interest. Perhaps these will be the topics for a future volume on philosophical criminology. However, what I hope is that this book has demonstrated the importance of further criminological consideration of values, morality, aesthetics, order/disorder, rules and respect; and perhaps also of an empathetic criminology.

References

ABC News (2015a) 'Prime Minister Malcolm Turnbull appeals for all Australians to show mutual respect following "brutal murder"', *ABC News Online*, 9 October, available at: www.abc.net.au/news/2015-10-09/malcolm-turnbull-plea-for-mutual-respect-after-parramatta-murder/6841892.

ABC News (2015b) 'Parramatta shooting: "If you don't like Australia, leave", Muslim leader tells worshippers', *ABC News Online*, 11 October, available at: www.abc.net.au/news/2015-10-09/if-you-dont-like-australia-leave-muslim-leader-tells-worshippers/6839886.

Albertson, K. and Fox, C. (2012) *Crime and Economics: An Introduction*, Abingdon: Routledge.

Aldred, N. (1995) 'Figure paintings and double portraits', in P. Melia (ed.) *David Hockney*, Manchester: Manchester University Press 68–88.

Alexander, S. and Ruderman, M. (1987) 'The role of procedural and distributive justice in organization behavior', *Social Justice Research*, 1(2) 177–98.

Amatrudo, A. (2009) *Criminology and Political Theory*, London: Sage.

Anderson, E. (1999) *Code of the Street: Decency, Violence and the Moral Life of the Inner City*, New York, NY: W.W. Norton and Co Inc.

Archer, M., Bhashkar, R., Collier, A., Lawson, T. and Norrie, A. (eds.) (1998) *Critical Realism: Essential Readings*, London: Routledge.

Arrigo, B.A. and Williams, C.R. (eds.) (2006) *Philosophy, Crime, and Criminology*, Urbana, IL: University of Illinois Press.

Artists and Illustrators (2013) 'Top 10 David Hockney quotes', *Artists and Illustrators*, 9 July, available at: www.artistsandillustrators.co.uk/news/unknown/911/top-10-david-hockney-quotes.

Ashworth, A., von Hirsch, A. and Roberts, J. (2009) *Principled Sentencing: Readings on Theory and Policy*, third edition, Oxford: Hart Publishing.

Atkinson, R. (2014) *Shades of Deviance (A Primer on Crime, Deviance and Social Harm)*, Abingdon: Routledge.

Austen, J. (1813/2003) *Pride and Prejudice*, London: Penguin Classics.

Austen, J. (1817/1995) *Northanger Abbey*, London: Penguin Classics.

Bachelard, G. (1969) *The Poetics of Space*, Boston, MA: Beacon Press.

Bagnoli, C. (2007) 'Respect and membership in the moral community', *Ethical Theory and Moral Practice*, 10(2) 113–28.

Banks, C. (2015) 'The importance of ethics in criminal justice', in M. Maguire and D. Okada (eds.) *Critical Issues in Criminal Justice: Thought, Policy and Practice*, second edition, Thousand Oaks, CA: Sage 9–32.

Banksy (2006) *Wall and Piece*, London: Century.

Bannister, J., Fyfe, N. and Kearns, A. (2006) 'Respectable or respectful? (In)civility and the city', *Urban Studies*, 43(5/6) 919–37.

Barthes, R. (1972) *Mythologies*, Translated by A. Lavers, New York NY: Hill and Wang.

Baumgardt, D. (1952) *Bentham and the Ethics of Today*, Princeton, NJ: Princeton University Press.

Becker, H. (1963) *Outsiders: Studies in the Sociology of Deviance*, New York, NY: The Free Press.

Becker, H. (1967) 'Whose side are we on?' *Social Problems*, 14(3) 239–47.

Beckett, K. and Herbert, S. (2010) *Banished: The New Social Control in Urban America*, New York, NY: Oxford University Press.

Beirne, P. (1987) 'Adolphe Quetelet and the origins of positivist criminology', *American Journal of Sociology*, 92(5) 1140–69.

Bennett, C. (2015) *What Is This Thing Called Ethics?* second edition, Abingdon: Routledge.

Bentham, J. (1825) *The Rationale of Reward*, London: John and H.L. Hunt.

Berman, M. (1982) *All That Is Solid Melts into Air: The Experience of Modernity*, New York, NY: Penguin.

Bhaskar, R. (1975) *A Realist Theory of Science*, Leeds: Leeds Books.

Blair, T. (1995) *Leader's speech, Brighton 1995*, available at: www. britishpoliticalspeech.org/speech-archive.htm?speech=201.

Blair, T. (2002) 'My vision for Britain', *The Guardian Online*, 10 November, available at: www.theguardian.com/politics/2002/nov/10/queensspeech2002.tonyblair.

Bosworth, M. and Hoyle, C. (2011) 'What is criminology? An introduction', in M. Bosworth and C. Hoyle (eds.) *What is Criminology?* Oxford: Oxford University Press 1–12.

Bottoms, A. (2002) 'Morality, crime, compliance and public policy', in A. Bottoms and M. Tonry (eds.) *Ideology, Crime and Criminal Justice: A Symposium in Honour of Sir Leon Radzinowicz*, Cullompton: Willan 20–53.

Bottoms, A. (2015) *Christianity and Crime*, Sermon at Trinity College Cambridge, 26 April, available at: http://trinitycollegechapel.com/media/filestore/sermons/2015-4-26-AnthonyBottoms.pdf.

Bottoms, A.E. and Preston, R.H. (eds.) (1980) *The Coming Penal Crisis: A Criminological and Theological Exploration*, Edinburgh: Scottish Academic Press.

Bourdieu, P. (1979/1984) *Distinction: A Social Critique of the Judgement of Taste* (translated by R. Nee) Cambridge, MA: Harvard University Press.

Bourgois, P. (1996) *In Search of Respect: Selling Crack in El Barrio*, Cambridge: Cambridge University Press.

Boutellier, H. (2000) *Crime and Morality: The Significance of Criminal Justice in Post-Modern Culture*, Dordrecht: Kluwer Academic Publishers.

Bowling, B. and Phillips, C. (2007) 'Disproportionate and discriminatory: Reviewing the evidence on police stop and search', *Modern Law Review*, 70(6) 936–61.

Braithwaite, J. (2000) 'Shame and criminal justice', *Canadian Journal of Criminology*, 42(3) 281–98.

Bratton, W.J. (1995) 'The New York City Police Department's civil enforcement of quality-of-life crimes', *Journal of Law and Policy* (Brooklyn Law School), 3(2) 447–64.

Brejzek, T. (2010) 'From social network to urban intervention: On the scenographies of flash mobs and urban swarms', *International Journal of Performance Arts and Digital Media*, 6(1) 111–24.

Brisman, A. (2010) '"Creative crime" and the phytological analogy', *Crime, Media, Culture*, 6(2) 205–25.

Brogden, M. and Ellison, G. (2013) *Policing in an Age of Austerity: A Postcolonial Perspective*, Abingdon: Routledge.

Brown, A. (2008) 'The war on "Neds": Media reports as evidence base', *Criminal Justice Matters*, 59, 16–17.

Brown, M. (2006) 'The aesthetics of crime', in B.A. Arrigo and C.R. Williams (eds.) *Philosophy, Crime, and Criminology*, Urbana and Chicago, IL: University of Illinois Press 223–56.

Butchvarov, P. (1989) *Scepticism in Ethics*, Bloomington, IN: Indiana University Press.

Cabanne, P. (1997) *Duchamp & Co.*, Paris: Terrail.

Cameron, D. (2010) 'David Cameron, leader of the Conservative Party, speaking at a rally in East Renfrewshire', 4 May, *Total Politics*, available at: www.totalpolitics.com/speeches/elections/general-election-2010/35353/david-cameron-leader-of-the-conservative-party-speaking-at-a-rally-in-east-renfrewshire.thtml.

Cameron, D. (2011) 'Speech on the fight-back after the riots', *New Statesman*, 15 August, available at: www.newstatesman.com/politics/2011/08/society-fight-work-rights.

Cameron, D. (2013) 'David Cameron eases China visa rules', *Daily Telegraph*, 3 December, available at: www.telegraph.co.uk/finance/china-business/10490692/David-Cameron-eases-China-visa-rules.html.

Cannadine, D. (1998) *Class in Britain*, London: Penguin.

Carlen, P. (2011) 'Against evangelism in academic criminology: For criminology as a scientific art', in M. Bosworth and C. Hoyle (eds.) *What is Criminology*, Oxford: Oxford University Press 95–108.

Carrabine, E. (2012) 'Just images: Aesthetics, ethics and visual criminology', *British Journal of Criminology*, 52(3) 463–89.

Carson, P.K. and Moser, T.L. (eds.) (2001) *Moral Relativism: A Reader*, New York, NY: Oxford University Press.

Carter, I. (2011) 'Respect and the basis of equality', *Ethics*, 121(3) 538–71.

Cazeaux, C. (ed.) (2011) *The Continental Aesthetics Reader*, second edition, Abingdon: Routledge.

Cheliotis, L (2010) 'The ambivalent consequences of visibility: Crime and prisons in the mass media', *Crime, Media, Culture*, 6(2) 169–84.

Chenery, S., Henshaw, C. and Pease, K. (1999) *Illegal Parking in Disabled Bays: A Means of Offender Targeting*, Police and Reducing Crime Briefing Note 1/99, London: Home Office.

Cicero (54–51BC/1928) *On the Republic On the Laws*, Translated by C.W. Keyes, Cambridge, MA: Harvard University Press.

Clarke, R.V. and Hough, M. (1984) *Crime and Police Effectiveness*, Home Office Research Study 79, London: Home Office.

Cockburn, B. (1983) *The Trouble with Normal*, Burlington, Ontario: True North Records.

Cohen, S. (1972) *Folk Devils and Moral Panics: The Creation of the Mods and Rockers*, London: MacGibbon and Kee Ltd.

Cohen, S. (1988) *Against Criminology*, New Brunswick, NJ: Transaction.

Comte, A. (1891) *Catechism of Positivism: Or Summary Exposition of the Universal Religion*, trans. R. Congreve, London: Kegan Paul, Trench Trübner and Co. Ltd..

The Conservative Party (2010) *Invitation to Join the Government of Britain: The Conservative Manifesto 2010*, London: The Conservative Party, available at: www.conservatives.com/~/media/Files/Manifesto2010

Costonis, J.J. (1989) *Icons and Aliens: Law, Aesthetics, and Environmental Change*, Urbana, IL: University of Illinois Press.

Crawford, A. and Lister, S. (2007) *The Use and Impact of Dispersal Orders: Sticking Plasters and Wake-up Calls*, Bristol: Policy Press.

Cray, E. (1972) *The Enemy in the Streets: Police Malpractice in America*, New York, NY: Anchor.

Cresswell, T. (1996) *In Place/Out of Place: Geography, Ideology and Transgression*, Minneapolis, MN: University of Minnesota Press.

Crewe, D. and Lippens, R. (eds.) (2015) *What is Criminology About? Philosophical Reflections*, Abingdon: Routledge.

Critchley, S. (2001) *Continental Philosophy: A Very Short Introduction*, Oxford: Oxford University Press.

Croall, H. (2016) 'Crimes of the powerful in Scotland', in H. Croall, G. Mooney and M. Munro (eds.) *Crime, Justice and Society in Scotland*, Abingdon: Routledge 131–48.

Cruickshank, D, (1973) 'Developers as vandals', in C. Ward (ed.) *Vandalism*, London: The Architectural Press 184–214.

Cunneen, C. and Tauri, J. (2016) *Indigenous Criminology*, Bristol: Policy Press.

Darwall, S.L. (1977) 'Two kinds of respect', *Ethics*, 88(1) 36–49.

Davis, M.H. (1994) *Empathy: A Social Psychological Approach*, Boulder, CO: Westview Press.

de Certeau, M. (1984) *The Practice of Everyday Life*, translated by Steven F. Rendall, Berkeley CA: University of California Press.

De Haan, W. (2003) 'Abolitionism and crime control', in E. McLaughlin, J. Muncie and G. Hughes (eds.) *Criminological Perspectives: Essential Readings*, Second Edition, London: Sage 381-92.

Devine, T.M. (1989) 'Social responses to agrarian "improvement": The Highland and Lowland Clearances in Scotland', in R.A. Houston and I.D. Whyte (eds.) *Scottish Society 1500–1800*, Cambridge: Cambridge University Press 148–68.

Ditton, J. (1977) *Part-time Crime: An Ethnography of Fiddling and Pilferage*, London: Macmillan.

Driver, J. (2007) *Ethics: The Fundamentals*, Malden, MA: Blackwell Publishing.

Duff, R.A. (1986) *Trials and Punishments*, Cambridge: Cambridge University Press.

Duff, R.A. (2010), 'Towards a Theory of Criminal Law?', *Aristotelian Society Supplementary Volume*, 84, 1–28.

Durkheim, É. (1893/2014) *The Division of Labor in Society*, Translation by W.D. Halls, New York, NY: Free Press.

Dworkin, R. (1977) *Taking Rights Seriously*, London: Duckworth.

Eco, U. (1979) *A Theory of Semiotics*, Bloomington, IN: Indiana University Press.

Edgerton, R.B. (1985) *Rules, Exceptions, and Social Order*, Berkeley, CA: University of California Press.

Ellis, A. (2012) *The Philosophy of Punishment*, Exeter: Imprint Academic.

Ericson, R.V. (1982) *Reproducing Order: A Study of Police Patrol Work*, Toronto: University of Toronto Press.

Erikson, K.T. (1966) *Wayward Puritans: A Study in the Sociology of Deviance*, New York, NY: Prentice Hall.

Feinberg, J. (1979) 'Civil disobedience in the modern world', *Humanities in Society*, 2(1) 37–60.

Feinberg, J. (1984) *Harm to Others: The Moral Limits of the Criminal Law*, New York, NY: Oxford University Press.

Feinberg, J. (1985) *Offense to Others: The Moral Limits of the Criminal Law*, New York, NY: Oxford University Press.

Feinberg, J. (1986) *Harm to Self: The Moral Limits of the Criminal Law Vol. 3.*, New York, NY: Oxford University Press.

Feinberg, J. (1990) *Harmless Wrongdoing: The Moral Limits of the Criminal Law Vol. 4.*, New York, NY: Oxford University Press.

Ferguson, A. (1767/1992) *An Essay on the History of Civil Society*, edited by F. Oz-Salzberger, Cambridge: Cambridge University Press.

Ferrell, J. (1996) *Crimes of Style: Urban Graffiti and the Politics of Criminality*, Boston, MA: Northeastern University Press.

Ferrell, J. (2006) 'The aesthetics of cultural criminology', in B.A. Arrigo and C.R. Williams (eds.) *Philosophy, Crime, and Criminology*, Urbana, IL: University of Illinois Press 257–78.

Ferrell, J. and Sanders, C.R. (1995) *Cultural Criminology*, Boston, MA: Northeastern University Press.

Finnis, J. (2011) *Natural Law and Natural Rights*, second edition, Oxford: Oxford University Press.

Foucault, M. (1977) *Discipline and Punish: The Birth of the Prison*, London: Penguin.

Francis, P. (2009) 'Visual criminology', *Criminal Justice Matters*, 78, 10–11.

Garland, D. (1990) *Punishment and Modern Society: A Study in Social Theory*, Oxford: Oxford University Press.

Garland, D. (2011) 'Criminology's place in the academic field', in M. Bosworth and C. Hoyle (eds.) *What is Criminology?* Oxford: Oxford University Press 298–317.

Garland, D. and Sparks, R. (2000) 'Criminology, social theory and the challenge of our times', *British Journal of Criminology*, 40(2) 189–204.

Geach, P.T. (1956) 'Good and evil', *Analysis*, 17(2) 33–42.

Gelsthorpe, L. (2015) 'A letter from our President', *British Society of Criminology Newsletter*, No. 76, Summer 2015, 6–7.

Gensler, H.J. and Tokmenko, M.G. (2004) 'Against cultural relativism', in H.J. Gensler, E.W. Spurgin and J.C. Swindal (eds.) *Ethics: Contemporary Readings*, Abingdon: Routledge 50–57.

Giddens, A. (1991) *Modernity and Self-identity: Self and Society in the Late Modern Age*, Stanford, CA: Stanford University Press.

Giddens, A. (1998) *The Third Way: The Renewal of Social Democracy*, Cambridge: Polity.

Gilpin, W. (1789) *Observations on the River Wye, and Several Parts of South Wales, & c.: Relative Chiefly to Picturesque Beauty: Made in the Summer of the Year 1770*, second edition, London: R. Blamire.

Gilpin, W. (1792) *Three Essays: On Picturesque Beauty, on Picturesque Travel and on Sketching Landscape: To Which is Added a Poem, on Landscape Painting*, London: R. Blamire.

Godfrey, B.S., Lawrence, P. and Williams, C.A. (2008) *History and Crime*, London: Sage.

Goffman, E. (1963) *Behavior in Public Places: Notes on the Social Organization of Gatherings*, New York, NY: The Free Press.

Goffman, E. (1967) *Interaction Ritual: Essays in Face to Face Behaviour*, Chicago, IL: Aldine.

Goffman, E. (1969) *Strategic Interaction*, Philadelphia, PA: University of Pennsylvania Press.

Goldman, E. (1925) *My Disillusionment in Russia*, London: C.W. Daniel.

Goode, E. and Ben-Yehuda, N. (2009) *Moral Panics: The Social Construction of Deviance*, Chichester: Wiley-Blackwell.

Gottfredson, M.R. (2011) 'Some advantages of a crime-free criminology', in M. Bosworth and C. Hoyle (eds.) *What is Criminology?* Oxford: Oxford University Press 35–48.

Green, L. (2012) 'Introduction', in H.L.A. Hart (ed.) *The Concept of Law*, third edition, Oxford: Oxford University Press xv–iv.

Greer, C. and McLaughlin, E. (2010) 'We predict a riot? Public order policing, new media environments and the rise of the citizen journalist', *British Journal of Criminology*, 50(6) 1041–59.

Greer, G. (2007) 'What should we do about graffiti?' *The Guardian*, 24 September, available at: www.theguardian.com/artanddesign/artblog/2007/sep/24/whatshouldwedoaboutgraffiti.

Griffin, J. (1996) *Value Judgement: Improving our Ethical Beliefs*, Oxford: Oxford University Press.

Groombridge, N. (2016) *Sports Criminology: A Critical Criminology of Sport and Games*, Bristol: Policy Press.

The Guardian (2013) 'Margaret Thatcher: A Life in Quotes', *The Guardian Online*, 8 April, available at: www.theguardian.com/politics/2013/apr/08/margaret-thatcher-quotes.

Halfacree, K.H. (1996) 'Out of place in the country: Travellers and the "rural idyll"', *Antipode*, 28(1) 42–72.

Hannerz, U. (1990) 'Cosmopolitans and locals in world culture', in M. Featherstone (ed.) *Global Culture*, London: Sage.

Hansen, S. (2015) '"Pleasure stolen from the poor": Community discourse on the "theft" of a Banksy', *Crime, Media, Culture*, Online First. DOI: 10.1177/1741659015612880.

Harcourt, B. (2001) *Illusion of Order: The False Promise of Broken Windows Policing*, Cambridge, MA: Harvard University Press.

Hart, H.L.A. (1961/2012) *The Concept of Law*, third edition, Oxford: Oxford University Press.

Havlin, L. (2010) 'Damien Hirst Touches Your Soul', *Dazed*, available at: www.dazeddigital.com/artsandculture/article/8710/1/damien-hirst-touches-your-soul

Hayek, F.A. (2013) *Law, Legislation and Liberty: A New Statement of the Liberal Principles of Justice and Political Economy*, Abingdon: Routledge.

Hayward, K. and Yar, M. (2006) 'The "Chav" phenomenon: Consumption, media and the construction of a new underclass', *Crime, Media, Culture*, 2(1) 9–28.

Hebdige, D. (1979) *Subculture: The Meaning of Style*, London: Methuen and Co Ltd.

Hechter, M. and Horne, C. (eds.) (2009) *Theories of Social Order*, second edition, Redwood City, CA: Stanford University Press.

Henry, S. (1978) *The Hidden Economy: The Context and Control of Borderline Crime*, London: Martin Robertson & Co.

Henry, S. and Milovanovic, D. (1996) *Constitutive Criminology: Beyond Postmodernism*, London: Sage.

Hermer, J. (2002) *Regulating Eden: The Nature of Order in North American Parks*, Toronto: University of Toronto Press.

Hertzler, J.O. (1934) 'On golden rules', *International Journal of Ethics*, 44(4) 418–36.

Hill, T.E. (2000) *Respect, Pluralism, and Justice: Kantian Perspectives*, Oxford: Oxford University Press.

Hillyard, P., Pantazis, C., Tombs, S. and Gordon, D. (eds.) (2004) *Beyond Criminology: Taking Harm Seriously*, London: Pluto Books.

Hinde, R.A. (2007) *Bending the Rules: The Flexibility of Absolutes in Modern Life*, Oxford: Oxford University Press.

Hobbes, T. (1651/1990) 'Leviathan', in S.M. Cahn (ed.) *Classics of Western Philosophy*, third edition, Cambridge, IN: Hackett Publishing Company 447–507.

Hough, M. (2010) 'Gold standard or fool's gold? The pursuit of certainty in experimental criminology', *Criminology and Criminal Justice*, 10(1) 11–22.

Hough, M., Jackson, J., Bradford, B., Myhill, A. and Quinton, P. (2010) 'Procedural justice, trust, and institutional legitimacy', *Policing: A Journal of Policy and Practice*, 4(3) 203–10.

Hume, D. (1739) *A Treatise of Human Nature: Being an Attempt to Introduce the Experimental Method of Reasoning into Moral Subjects*, London: John Noon.

Hume, D. (1757) *Four Dissertations. I The Natural History of Religion. II Of the Passions. III Of Tragedy. IV Of the Standard of Taste*, London: A. Millar.

Husak, D. (2008) *Overcriminalization: The Limits of the Criminal Law*, Oxford: Oxford University Press.

Innes, M. and Fielding, N. (2002) 'From community to communicative policing: "Signal crimes" and the problem of public reassurance,' *Sociological Research Online*, 7(2) available at: www.socresonline.org. uk/7/2/innes.html

The Jackdaw (2015) 'Who did it? Not Duchamp! A Conceptual Inconvenience', *The Jackdaw*, September, available at: www. thejackdaw.co.uk/wp-content/uploads/2015/09/Duchamp-Fountain-II1.pdf.

Jacobs, J. (1961/1992) *The Death and Life of Great American Cities*, New York, NY: Vintage Books.

James, Z. (2015) 'Policing hate against Gypsies and Travellers: Dealing with the dark side', in N. Chakraborti and J. Garland (eds.) *Responding to Hate Crime: The Case for Connecting Policy and Research*, Bristol: Policy Press 215–29.

Jewkes, Y. and Moran, D. (2014) 'Should prison architecture be brutal, bland or beautiful?' *Scottish Justice Matters*, 2(1) 8–10.

Johnson, S.D. and Bowers, K.J. (2003) 'Opportunity is in the eye of the beholder: The role of publicity in crime prevention', *Criminology and Public Policy*, 2(3) 497–524.

Kant, I. (1785/1990) 'Grounding for the metaphysics of morals', in S.M. Cahn (ed.) *Classics of Western Philosophy*, third edition, Indianapolis, IN: Hackett 1009–58.

Kant, I. (1790/2011) 'Extracts from "Analytic of Aesthetic Judgment; and "Dialectic of Aesthetic Judgment', Critique of Judgment', in C. Cazeaux (ed.) *The Continental Aesthetics Reader*, Second Edition, Abingdon: Routledge 3-39.

Karstedt, S. and Farrall, S. (2006) 'The moral economy of everyday crime: Markets, consumers and citizens', *British Journal of Criminology*, 46(6) 1011–36.

Kelsen, H. (1934/1967) *Pure Theory of Law*, Translated by M. Knight, Berkeley, CA: University of California Press.

Knepper, P. (2007) *Criminology and Social Policy*, London: Sage.

Knepper, P. and Ystehede, P.J. (eds.) (2013) *The Cesare Lombroso Handbook*, Abingdon: Routledge.

Korsmeyer, C. (2005). 'Taste', in B. Gaut and D. McIver Lopes (eds.) *The Routledge Companion to Aesthetics*, second edition, Abingdon: Routledge 267–79.

Kraut, R. (2011) *Against Absolute Goodness*, Oxford: Oxford University Press.

Kubrin, C.E. (2008) 'Making order of disorder: A call for conceptual clarity', *Criminology and Public Policy*, 7(2) 203–14.

Lamont, W.D. (1955) *The Value Judgement*, Edinburgh: Edinburgh University Press.

Lawrence, D.H. (1929/1977) 'Ugliness': from 'Nottingham and the Mining Country', in A. Clayre (ed.) *Nature and Industrialization*, Oxford: Oxford University Press 387–91.

Laycock, G. (2005) 'Defining crime science', in M.J. Smith and N. Tilley (eds.) *Crime Science: New Approaches to Preventing and Detecting Crime*, Cullompton: Willan 3–24.

Lefebvre, H. (2000), *Everyday Life in the Modern World*, translated by S. Rabinovitch, London: Continuum.

Lemos, R.M. (1995) *The Nature of Value: Axiological Investigations*, Gainesville, FL: University Press of Florida.

Lewis, C.S. (1952) *Mere Christianity*, London: Collins.

Lind, E.A. and Tyler, T.R. (1988) *The Social Psychology of Procedural Justice*, New York, NY: Plenum Press.

Lippens, R. and Crewe, D. (eds.) (2011) *Existentialist Criminology*, Abingdon: Routledge.

Loader, I. and Sparks, R. (2011) *Public Criminology?* Abingdon: Routledge.

Locke, J. (1689/1995) *An Essay Concerning Human Understanding*, Amherst, NY: Prometheus Books.

Lorand, R. (2000) *Aesthetic Order: A Philosophy of Order, Beauty and Art*, Abingdon: Routledge.

Lorenz, E. (2000) 'The butterfly effect', in R. Abraham and Y. Ueda (eds.) *The Chaos Avant-garde: Memories of the Early Days of Chaos Theory*, Singapore: World Scientific 91–4.

Loury, G., Karlan, P., Shelby, T. and Wacquant, L. (2008) *Race, Incarceration, and American Values*, Boston, MA: Massachusetts Institute of Technology.

Lull, J. (2000) *Media, Communication, Culture: A Global Approach*, Cambridge: Polity Press.

Lyons, D. (1976) 'Ethical relativism and the problem of incoherence', *Ethics*, 86(2) 107–21.

Lyotard, J.-F. (1984) *The Postmodern Condition: A Report on Knowledge*, translated by G. Bennington and B. Massumi, Manchester: University of Manchester Press.

Mackie, J.L. (1977) *Ethics: Inventing Right and Wrong*, Harmondsworth: Pelican.

May, T. (2011) *Theresa May Speech in Full*, 4 October, available at: www.politics.co.uk/comment-analysis/2011/10/04/theresa-may-speech-in-full.

McDonald, H.P. (2004) *Radical Axiology: A First Philosophy of Values*, Amsterdam: Editions Rodopi BV.

Merton, R.K. (1938) 'Social structure and anomie', *American Sociological Review*, 3(5) 672–82.

Mill, J.S. (1859/2002) *On Liberty*, Mineola, NY: Dover Publications.

Millie, A. (2006) 'Anti-social behaviour: Concerns of minority and marginalised Londoners', *Internet Journal of Criminology*, available at: www.internetjournalofcriminology.com/Millie%20-%20Anti-social%20Behaviour.pdf.

Millie, A. (2008) 'Anti-social behaviour, behavioural expectations and an urban aesthetic', *British Journal of Criminology*, 48(3) 379–94.

Millie, A. (2009a) *Anti-Social Behaviour*, Maidenhead: Open University Press.

Millie, A. (ed.) (2009b) *Securing Respect: Behavioural Expectations and Anti-Social Behaviour in the UK*, Bristol: Policy Press.

Millie, A. (2009c) 'Respect and city living: Urban contest or cosmopolitanism?' in A. Millie (ed.) *Securing Respect: Behavioural Expectations and Anti-Social Behaviour in the UK*, Bristol: Policy Press 193–215.

Millie, A. (2010) 'Moral politics, moral decline and anti-social behaviour', *People, Place and Policy Online*, 4(1) 6–13.

Millie, A. (2011) 'Value judgments and criminalization', *British Journal of Criminology*, 51(2) 278–95.

Millie, A. (2012) 'Police stations, architecture and public reassurance', *British Journal of Criminology*, 52(6) 1092–112.

Millie, A. (2013) 'The policing task and the expansion (and contraction) of British policing', *Criminology and Criminal Justice*, 13(2) 143–60.

Millie, A. (2014a) 'Reassurance policing and signal crimes', in G. Bruinsma and D. Weisburd (eds.) *Encyclopedia of Criminology and Criminal Justice*, New York, NY: Springer 4327–35.

Millie, A. (2014b) 'The aesthetics of anti-social behaviour', in S. Pickard (ed.) *Anti-Social Behaviour in Britain: Victorian and Contemporary Perspectives*, Basingstoke: Palgrave Macmillan 102–11.

Millie, A. (2016) 'Urban interventionism as a challenge to aesthetic order: Towards an aesthetic criminology', *Crime, Media, Culture*. Online First. DOI: 10.1177/1741659016631609.

Millie, A. and Herrington, V. (2005) 'Bridging the gap: Understanding reassurance policing', *Howard Journal of Criminal Justice*, 44(1) 41–56.

Millie, A., Jacobson, J., McDonald, E. and Hough, M. (2005) *Anti-Social Behaviour Strategies: Finding a Balance*, Bristol: Policy Press.

Milovanovic, D. (1997) *Chaos, Criminology, and Social Justice: The New Orderly (Dis)Order*, Westport, CO: Praeger.

Mitchell, D. (2001) 'Postmodern geographical praxis? Postmodern impulse and the war against homeless people in the "Post-Justice" city', in C. Minca (ed.) *Postmodern Geography: Theory and Praxis*, Oxford: Blackwell 57–92.

Mitchell, D. (2003) *The Right to the City: Social Justice and the Fight for Public Space*, New York, NY: Guilford Press.

Moore, G.E. (1903/2005) *Principia Ethica*, New York, NY: Barnes and Noble.

Moore, M.S. (1992) 'Law as a functional kind', in R.P. George (ed.) *Natural Law Theory: Contemporary Essays*, Oxford: Clarendon Press 188–243.

Moore, S. (2008) Street life, neighbourhood policing and "the community", in P. Squires (ed.) *ASBO Nation: The Criminalisation of Nuisance*, Bristol: Policy Press 179–201.

Mumford, L. (1961) *The City in History: Its Origins, its Transformations, and its Prospects*, New York, NY: Harcourt, Brace and World.

Newman, O. (1972) *Defensible Space: People and Design in the Violent City*, London: Architectural Press.

Nietzsche, F. (1886/2003) *Beyond Good and Evil: Prelude to a Philosophy of the Future*, Tr. R.J. Hollingdale, London: Penguin Books.

Obama, B. (2007) *The Audacity of Hope: Thoughts on Reclaiming the American Dream*, Edinburgh: Canongate Books Ltd.

Obama, B. (2010) *Remarks by the President in State of the Union Address*, 27 January, available at: www.whitehouse.gov/the-press-office/remarks-president-state-union-address.

O'Brien, M. and Penna, S. (2007) 'Review essay: Critical criminology: Continuity and change', *Criminal Justice Review*, 32(3) 246–55.

Olson, J. (2015) 'Doubts about intrinsic value', in I. Hirose and J. Olson (eds.) *The Oxford Handbook of Value Theory*, Oxford: Oxford University Press 44–59.

O'Neill, M. and Seal, L. (2012) *Transgressive Imaginations: Crime, Deviance and Culture*, Basingstoke: Palgrave Macmillan.

Oxley, J.C. (2011) *The Moral Dimensions of Empathy: Limits and Applications in Ethical Theory and Practice*, Basingstoke: Palgrave Macmillian.

Pearson, G. (1983) *Hooligan: A History of Respectable Fears*, Basingstoke: Macmillan.

Pearson, G. (2009) '"A Jekyll in the classroom, a Hyde in the street": Queen Victoria's Hooligans', in A. Millie (ed.) *Securing Respect: Behavioural Expectations and Anti-Social Behaviour in the UK*, Bristol: Policy Press 41–71.

Perry, R.B. (1926/2007) *General Theory of Value*, Oxford: Oxford University Press.

Polizzi, D. (2016) *A Philosophy of the Social Construction of Crime*, Bristol: Policy Press.

Popper, K. (1945) *The Open Society and its Enemies: Volume 1. The Spell of Plato*, London: George Routledge & Sons Ltd.

Presdee, M. (2000) *Cultural Criminology and the Carnival of Crime*, London: Routledge.

Pruesse, K. (ed.) (1999) *Accidental Audience: Urban Interventions by Artists*, Toronto: off\site collective.

Putnam, R. (2000) *Bowling Alone: The Collapse and Revival of American Community*, New York, NY: Simon and Schuster.

Rackham, O. (1990) *Trees and Woodland in the British Landscape: The Complete History of Britain's Trees, Woods and Hedgerows*, London: Phoenix Press.

Radzinowicz, L. (1966) *Ideology and Crime: A Study of Crime in its Social and Historical Context*, London: Heinemann Educational Books Ltd.

Raz, J. (2009) *The Authority of Law: Essays on Law and Morality*, second edition, Oxford: Oxford University Press.

Reiner, R. (1992) 'Policing a postmodern society', *Modern Law Review*, 55(6) 761–81.

Reiner, R. (2013) 'Who governs? Democracy, plutocracy, science and prophecy in policing', *Criminology and Criminal Justice*, 13(2) 161–80.

Respect Task Force (2006) *Respect Action Plan*, London: Home Office.

Ricoeur, P. (1990) 'The Golden Rule: Exegetical and theological perplexities', *New Testament Studies*, 36(3) 392–7.

Rifkin, J. (2009) *The Empathic Civilization: The Race to Global Consciousness in a World in Crisis*, London: Penguin.

Roberts, R. (1971/1990) *The Classic Slum: Salford Life in the First Quarter of the Century*, London: Penguin.

Rønnow-Rasmussen, T. (2015) 'Intrinsic and extrinsic value', in I. Hirose and J. Olson (eds.) *The Oxford Handbook of Value Theory*, Oxford: Oxford University Press 29–43.

Rønnow-Rasmussen, T. and Zimmerman, M.J. (eds.) (2005) *Recent Works on Intrinsic Value*, Dordrecht: Springer.

Ross, W.D. (1930/2002), *The Right and the Good* (ed. P. Stratton-Lake), Oxford: Clarendon Press.

Rousseau, J.-J. (1762/2003) *On the Social Contract*, translated by G.D.H. Cole, Mineola, NY: Dover Publications Inc.

Ruskin, J. (1857) *The Seven Lamps of Architecture*, New York, NY: Wiley and Halsted.

Russell, B. (1967) *The Autobiography of Bertrand Russell, 1872–1914*, Toronto: McClelland and Stewart.

Saito, Y. (2007) *Everyday Aesthetics*, Oxford: Oxford University Press.

Sampson, R.J. (2010) 'Gold standard myths: Observations on the experimental turn in quantitative criminology', *Journal of Quantitative Criminology*, 26(4) 489–500.

Sampson, R.J. and Raudenbush, S.W. (1999) 'Systematic social observation of public spaces: A new look at disorder in urban neighbourhoods', *American Journal of Sociology*, 105(3) 603–51.

Sandercock, L. (2003) *Cosmopolis II: Mongrel Cities of the 21st Century*, London: Continuum.

Schellenkens, E. (2007) *Aesthetics and Morality*, London: Continuum.

Schofield, P., Pease-Watkin, C. and Blamires, C. (eds.) (2002) *Rights, Representation, and Reform: Nonsense upon Stilts and Other Writings on the French Revolution (The Collected Works of Jeremy Bentham)*, Oxford: Clarendon Press.

Scott, N. and Seglow, J. (2007) *Altruism*, Maidenhead: Open University Press.

Scraton, P. (2005) *The Authoritarian Within: Reflections on Power, Knowledge and Resistance*, Inaugural Lecture at Queens University Belfast, 9 June, available at: www.statewatch.org/news/2005/nov/phil-scraton-inaugural-lecture.pdf.

Scruton, R. (2009) *Beauty*, Oxford: Oxford University Press.

Sennett, R. (1970) *The Uses of Disorder: Personal Identity and City Life*, New York, NY: W.W. Norton.

Sennett, R. (2003) *Respect: The Formation of Character in an Age of Inequality*, London: Penguin Books.

Sennett, R. (2006) 'Views on respect: Richard Sennett', *BBC News Online*, 9 January, available at: http://news.bbc.co.uk/1/hi/uk/4589616.stm.

Sentamu, J. (2006) 'View of respect: Archbishop of York', BBC News Online, 9 January, available at: http://news.bbc.co.uk/1/hi/uk/4589636.stm.

Shapland, J. and Bottoms, A. (2011) 'Reflections on social values, offending and desistance among young adult recidivists', *Punishment and Society*, 13(3) 256–82.

Shearing, C. (2015) 'Criminology and the anthropocene', *Criminology and Criminal Justice*, 15(2) 255–69.

Sibley, S. (1995) *Geographies of Exclusion*, London: Routledge.

Sim, S. (ed.) (2011) *The Lyotard Dictionary*, Edinburgh: Edinburgh University Press.

Simon, J., Temple, N. and Tobe, R. (2013) *Architecture and Justice: Judicial Meanings in the Public Realm*, Farnham: Ashgate.

Slovic, P. (1992) 'Perceptions of risk: Reflections on the psychometric paradigm', in S. Krimsky and D. Goulding (eds.) *Social Theories of Risk*, Westport, CT: Praeger 117-52.

Smart, J.J.B. (1973) 'An outline of a system of utilitarian ethics', in J.J.C. Smart and B. Williams (eds.) *Utilitarianism: For and Against*, Cambridge: Cambridge University Press.

Smith, A. (1776) *An Inquiry into the Nature and Causes of the Wealth of Nations*, London: W. Strahan and T. Cadell.

Smith, B., Albert, H., Armstrong, D., Barcan Marcus, R., Campbell, K., Glauser, R., Haller, R., Mugnai, M., Mulligan, K., Peña, L., van Orman Quine, Röd, W., Schuhmann, K., Schulthess, D., Simons, P., Thom, R., Willard, D. and Wolenski, J. (1992) 'From Professor Barry Smith and others', *The Times*, Letters, 9 May, available at: http://ontology.buffalo.edu/smith/varia/Derrida_Letter.htm.

Smith, N. (1996) *The New Urban Frontier: Gentrification and the Revanchist City*, London: Routledge.

Smith, P. (2008) *Moral and Political Philosophy: Key Issues, Concepts and Theories*, Basingstoke: Palgrave Macmillan.

Snyder, G.J. (2009) *Graffiti Lives: Beyond the Tag in New York's Urban Underground*, New York, NY: New York University Press.

Spitzer, S. (1975) 'Toward a Marxian theory of deviance', *Social Problems*, 22(5) 638–51.

Squires, P. (2009) '"You lookin' at me?" Discourses of respect and disrespect, identity and violence', in A. Millie (ed.) *Securing Respect: Behavioural Expectations and Anti-Social Behaviour in the UK*, Bristol: Policy Press 239–65.

Staeheli, L. and Mitchell, D. (2008) *The People's Property?: Power, Politics and the Public*, New York, NY: Routledge.

Stedman Jones, D. (2014) *Masters of the Universe: Hayek, Friedman, and the Birth of Neoliberal Politics*, Princeton, NJ: Princeton University Press.

Sturgeon, N.L. (1994) 'Moral disagreement and moral relativism', *Social Philosophy and Policy*, 11(1) 80–115.

Sumner, W.G. (1906/1940) *Folkways: A Study of the Sociological Importance of Usages, Manners, Customs Mores and Morals*, Boston, MA: Ginn and Company.

Sutherland, E. and Cressey, D. (1955) *Principles of Criminology*, fifth edition, Chicago, IL: Lippencott.

Swedberg, R. (2001) 'Sociology and game theory: Contemporary and historical perspectives', *Theory and Society*, 30(3) 301–35.

Taylor, I., Walton, P. and Young, J. (1973) *The New Criminology: For a Social Theory of Deviance*, Abingdon: Routledge.

Thom, R. (1975) 'La Théorie des catastrophes: État présent et perspectives', in A. Manning (ed.) *Dynamical Systems – Warwick 1974: Proceedings of a Symposium Held at the University of Warwick, 1973/74 (Lecture Notes in Mathematics: 468)*, Berlin: Springer-Verlag 366–72.

Thomson, J.J. (1997) 'The right and the good', *The Journal of Philosophy*, 94(6) 273–98.

Thomson, J.J. (2001) *Goodness and Advice*, Ed. By A. Gutmann, Princeton NJ: Princeton University Press.

Thrift, N. (2004) 'Intensities of feeling: Towards a spatial politics of affect', *Geografiska Annaler: Series B, Human Geography*, 86(1) 57–78.

Thrift, N. (2005) 'But malice aforethought: Cities and the natural history of hatred', *Transactions, Institute of British Geographers*, 30(2) 133-50.

Titchmarsh, A. (2003) *Royal Gardeners: The History of Britain's Royal Gardens*, London: Random House.

Tonry, M. (ed.) (2014) *Why Crime Rates Fall and Why They Don't*, Crime and Justice: A Review of Research Volume 43, Chicago, IL: University of Chicago Press.

Tovey, A. (2015) 'Donald Trump: "Windfarms are ruining the landscape"', *The Telegraph*, 8 June, available at: www.telegraph.co.uk/finance/newsbysector/constructionandproperty/11661281/Donald-Trump-Windfarms-are-ruining-the-landscape.html.

Treadwell, J. (2008) '"Call the (fashion) police": How fashion became criminalised', *Papers from the British Criminology Conference*, (8), 117–33.

Truss, L. (2005) *Talk to the Hand: The Utter Bloody Rudeness of Everyday Life (or Six Good Reasons to Stay Home and Bolt the Door)*, London: Profile Books.

Tuan, Y.-F (1974) *Topophilia: A Study of Environmental Perception, Attitudes and Values*, Englewood Cliffs, NJ: Prentice-Hall.

Turner, T. (2013) *British Gardens: History, Philosophy and Design*, Abingdon: Routledge.

Valverde, M. (2012) *Everyday Law on the Street: City Governance in an Age of Diversity*, Chicago, IL: University of Chicago Press.

Valverde, M. (2013) Time and space in the governance of crime and security. *Criminology and Criminal Justice Journal Lecture for 2013*, Leeds, 16 October.

Valverde, M. (2014) 'Studying the governance of crime and security: Space, time and jurisdiction', *Criminology and Criminal Justice*, 14(4) 379–91.

Walsh, A. (2009) *Biology and Criminology: The Biosocial Synthesis*, New York, NY: Routledge.

Wander, P. (2000) 'Introduction to the Transaction Edition', in H. Lefebvre, *Everyday Life in the Modern World*, translated by S. Rabinovitch, London: Continuum vii–xxiii.

Ward, C. (1973) 'Planners as vandals', in C. Ward (ed.) *Vandalism*, London: The Architectural Press 173–83.

Weisburd, D.L., Goff, E.R. and Yang, S-M. (2012) *The Criminology of Place: Street Segments and Our Understanding of the Crime Problem*, Oxford: Oxford University Press.

Wellman C. (1975) *Morals and Ethics*, Glenview, IL: Scott, Foresman and Company.

Wells, H. (2012) *The Fast and the Furious: Drivers, Speed Cameras and Control in a Risk Society*, Farnham: Ashgate.

Wheeldon, J. (2015) 'Ontology, epistemology, and irony: Richard Rorty and re-imagining pragmatic criminology', *Theoretical Criminology*, 19(3) 396–415.

Whyte, D. (2009) *Crimes of the Powerful: A Reader*, Maidenhead: Open University Press.

Williams, C.R. and Arrigo, B.A. (2006) 'Introduction: Philosophy, crime, and theoretical criminology', in B.A. Arrigo and C.R. Williams (eds.) *Philosophy, Crime, and Criminology*, Urbana and Chicago, IL: University of Illinois Press 1–38.

Wilson, J.Q. and Kelling, G.L. (1982) 'Broken windows: The police and neighborhood safety' *The Atlantic Monthly*, 249(3) 29–38.

Wirth, L. (1931) 'Culture conflict and delinquency, I. Culture conflict and misconduct', *Social Forces*, 9(4) 484–92.

Young, A. (2010) 'Negotiated consent or zero tolerance? Responding to graffiti and street art in Melbourne', *City*, 14(1/2) 99–114.

Young, A. (2012) 'Criminal images: The affective judgment of graffiti and street art', *Crime, Media, Culture*, 8(3) 297–314.

Young, A. (2014) *Street Art, Public City: Law, Crime and the Urban Imagination*, Abingdon: Routledge.

Young, J. (1981) 'Thinking Seriously about Crime: Some Models of Criminology', in M. Fitzgerald, G. McLennan and J. Pawson (eds.) *Crime and Society: Readings in History and Theory*, London: Routledge.

Young, J. (2003) 'In praise of dangerous thoughts', *Punishment and Society*, 5(1) 97–107.

Zaki, J. and Ochsner, K.N. (2012) 'The neuroscience of empathy: Progress, pitfalls and promise', *Nature Neuroscience*, 15, 675–80.

Zimmerman, M.J. (2015) 'Value and normativity', in I. Hirose and J. Olson (eds.) *The Oxford Handbook of Value Theory*, Oxford: Oxford University Press 13–28.

Žižek, S. (2008) *Violence*, London: Profile Books.

Zukin, S. (1995) *The Culture of Cities*, Oxford: Blackwell.

Index